The
TEA
CYCLOPEDIA

The
TEA
CYCLOPEDIA
A Celebration of the World's Favorite Drink

Dr. Keith Souter

SKYHORSE PUBLISHING

Skyhorse Publishing books may be purchased in bulk at special
discounts for sales promotion, corporate gifts, fund-raising, or educational purposes. Special editions can also be created to specifications.
For details, contact the Special Sales Department, Skyhorse Publishing,
307 West 36th Street, 11th Floor, New York, NY 10018 or
info@skyhorsepublishing.com.

Skyhorse® and Skyhorse Publishing® are registered trademarks of
Skyhorse Publishing, Inc.®, a Delaware corporation.

Visit our website at www.skyhorsepublishing.com.

10 9 8 7 6 5 4 3 2 1

Library of Congress Cataloging-in-Publication Data
Souter, Keith M.
 The tea cyclopedia : a celebration of the world's favorite drink / Keith
Souter.
    pages cm
  ISBN 978-1-62636-091-4 (hardcover : alk. paper) 1. Tea--History-
-Encyclopedias. 2. Tea--Social aspects--Encyclopedias. I. Title.
  GT2905.S64 2013
  394.1'503--dc23
                              2013027917

Printed in the United States of America

For Ruth, who knows how to make a great cup of tea.
With happy memories of many pots shared together.

Contents

I am a hardened and shameless tea-drinker, who has for twenty years diluted his meals with only the infusion of this fascinating plant, whose kettle scarcely has time to cool, who with tea amuses the evening, with tea solaces the midnights, and with tea welcomes the morning.

Dr. Samuel Johnson (1709–1784)

A Personal Toast to Judge Dee, a Great Tea Drinker

I ADORE TEA.

There, I admit this from the start. I have enjoyed drinking tea all my life in all of its forms, and as a doctor, I have kept an avid interest in the research that keeps coming out and which suggests that the ancient Chinese were quite correct in their assertion that tea is an herb with great medicinal potential.

In addition to being a doctor, I am a teller of mysteries, a crime writer. I write "cozy" detective stories in the tradition of Agatha Christie and young adult mysteries set during the Victorian era, which were inspired by reading stories about Sherlock Holmes by Sir Arthur Conan Doyle. Yet my greatest influence as a writer was a Dutch diplomat by the name of Robert van Gulik. I first discovered one of his novels in a market in a sleepy English town when I was twelve years old. The book was *The Chinese Maze Murders*, a novel about the real-life Tang dynasty master-detective Judge Dee.

I loved that book and its rich descriptions of life in China in the seventh century. It certainly shaped my reading interests for many years, and it inspired me to become a mystery writer myself. Even as I sit here in my study penning these words with a pot of oolong tea by my side, I am transported back to those amazing times, to the orange grove where the great detective sips tea and works out the trail of clues that lead him to solve the case.

Tea was an important part of Judge Dee's life, just as it has been an integral part of mine. I have studied tea in all its forms and functions, written about it many times in my weekly newspaper column, and, like Robert van Gulik, have woven it into my own crime novels. My Scottish detective, Inspector Torquil McKinnon, is a tea enthusiast, as are most of the good folk of West Uist, the Outer Hebridean island on which my novels are set. Yet in the back of my mind I wanted to do more than write about tea in passing. I had a desire to write a book that would be a toast to this great drink that the ancient Chinese gave to the world. And now, with *The Tea Cyclopedia*, I thank the Emperor Shen Nong for discovering tea, and I thank Robert van Gulik and Judge Dee Djeng for being the first to infuse my interest in tea.

Keith Souter
Wakefield, UK

Pre-taste

TEA IS THE MOST POPULAR DRINK IN THE WORLD, NEXT to water. That might sound rather amazing, yet it's true. More tea is drunk than all the coffee, cocoa, soft drinks, and alcohol put together. That means a lot of people are drinking it in countries around the world, every second of the day.

The United Kingdom is one of the largest per capita tea-drinking nations in the world. According to the United Kingdom Tea Council, the British consume a staggering 60.2 billion cups a year, each person drinking on average four cups a day.[1] People in the Republic of Ireland drink even more, averaging four to six cups. Yet this is nothing in comparison to Turkey, where the average is ten to fifteen cups a day. And of course, the United States doesn't do too badly either. It is estimated that 80 percent of households have tea in their cupboards, and on any day, about one half of the American population drinks tea.[2] The majority of this is taken as black iced tea, the first great tea innovation that America gave to the world, and 65 percent of the tea consumed worldwide is made with that other great American invention, the tea bag.

China is the largest tea producer in the world, and Japan is renowned for its tea ceremony, yet they are surprisingly low in their tea consumption. Neither is in the top ten tea-drinking countries in the world.

There are over 1,500 different teas to choose from, produced by 25 tea-growing nations. That means that there are a whole lot of different flavors to choose from. Yet apart from its flavor there seem to be many reasons for tea's popularity. Tea drinking is almost a way of life for vast numbers of people. It is a love, an addiction, and even a philosophy. Tea has united people in times of adversity, yet it has also divided nations, caused revolutions, and indirectly led to wars. It is therefore probably true to say that many storms have had their origin in the teacups of the world.

Different cultures have developed their own ways of drinking this beloved beverage and have created various rituals of tea drinking—from the highly organized Japanese tea ceremony, which can take several hours, to the brewing of the chai urn in rural India, to the quick mashing of the morning cuppa in Britain. All of these methods are not only fascinating, but can also be great fun to experiment with. Not only that, but for centuries, tea has been extolled as a health giving drink. Now, medical science has started to put these alleged health giving qualities to the test—with very encouraging results.

The book naturally falls into three parts. Part One is about the history of tea, from its beginnings in China and its spread around the world to its use as a precious taxable commodity and its counterpart as black market contraband that has fuelled skirmishes, battles, and wars. Part Two delves into taking tea, the rituals and ceremonies, and some of the accompaniments that go well with this wonderful drink. Finally, Part Three tackles the uses of tea as a drink that may have benefits for your health, its use in cocktails, some science experiments that you can conduct in the comfort of your own kitchen, and—if you are curious about the future—a chapter on *tasseography*, or teacup fortune-telling. This tea cyclopedia may do more than whet your appetite for tea; it may begin a complete obsession.

The
TEA
CYCLOPEDIA

PART ONE

THE HISTORY OF TEA

Chapter One

The Name for Tea

What's in a name? that which we call a rose
By any other name would smell as sweet;
　　　　　　　　　William Shakespeare (1564–1616), Romeo and Juliet

IN ENGLISH, TEA IS A NEAT, SHORT WORD, BUT IT HAS BEEN spelled differently throughout its long history. It has been called tea, tee, tcha, chaw, and other variants. Its origin is actually quite interesting and has been extensively studied by linguistic scholars as it reflects the plant and the way that the drink spread across the world.[3]

There are, in fact, two families of words that are used around the world, which come from the way that the Chinese character for tea has been pronounced:

茶 this is the written character for tea

茶 this is the calligraphic representation for tea

The character for tea indicated above has been in use since at least the third century. It is used in both standard Cantonese and Mandarin written Chinese, yet it has two pronunciations. In the Mandarin language, it is pronounced *cha*. In the Amoy dialect, which is spoken in the Fujian province and Taiwan, it is pronounced *tay*.

Mainland provinces tend to use Canton and Mandarin dialects, and coastal provinces use the Minnan dialects (which includes the Amoy).

The fascinating part of all of this is that the two words spread in entirely different fashions. Sometimes, they came back together again, as different cultures who were introduced to one word meet another where the other word was used. For example, in England, a "cup of tea" is the polite way of referring to a drink of tea, whereas a "cup of char" is the more homely vernacular. Char comes from the Indian use of the word (tea is "chai" in India), which was absorbed into the English language by British soldiers serving in India in the nineteenth century.

The *Cha* Route

From China, tea went to Japan under the name of *cha*. It reached Persia as cha, but became modified in Arabic to become *chai*. Similarly, in Turkey it became *chay*.

In 1638, when Tsar Michel I of Russia was given a consignment of four poods* of tea by a Mongolian ruler, it went by the name of chai. And when it went to India, Bangladesh, Pakistan, and Sri Lanka, it rejoiced in its traditional name of cha.

The *Tay* Way

The *tay* name spread around the world later than its cha counterpart. It was towards the end of the Ming dynasty, in 1644, that British traders first came across tea when they set up trading posts in Xiamen in the province of Fujian, in Southeast China. The local people of Xiamen spoke in the Fujian dialect and used the word tay, which the British spelled as tea. And this is the word that has spread around the English speaking countries of the world, which traded with Britain.

It's important to know the word for tea wherever you are in the world. Here are the words and the derivations from the two words *cha* and *tay*:

---

* A "pood" was a Russian measure of weight, roughly equivalent to around thirty-five pounds.

Languages Using the Tay Derivative	
Afrikaans	tee
Czech	té or thé
Danish	te
Dutch	thee
English	tea
Esperanto	teo
Finnish	tee
German	tee
Greek	téïon
Hebrew	te
Hungarian	tea
Indonesian	the
Italian	tè, thè or the
Javanese	tèh
Latin	thea (but, of course, tea was never known to the Romans!)
Latvian	tēja
Malay	the
Maltese	tè
Norwegian	te
Spanish	té
Sundanese (Java)	entèh
Swedish	te

Languages Using the Cha Derivative	
Albanian	çaj
Arabic	chai or shai
Aramaic	chai
Assamese	sah
Bangla	cha
Bosnian	čaj
Bulgarian	chai
English vernacular	char
Gujarati	cha
Hindi	chay
Japanese	cha, sa
Khasi	sha
Korean	cha
Lao	saa
Malayalam	chaaya
Mongolian	tsai
Punjabi	chāh
Portuguese	chá
Serbian	čaj
Somali	shah
Swahili	chai
Tibetan	ja
Turkish	chay
Urdu	chai
Vietnamese	rà and chè

Chapter Two

The Gift of Tea

So where and when did this worldwide love affair with tea begin?
In China, many eons ago.
Back in the mists of antiquity when the Emperor Shen Nong ruled.
Or so it is said.

The Leaves That Fell Before the Divine Farmer

FOR A DRINK THAT IS SO POPULAR AND THAT HAS SUCH A long tradition, it is important to pinpoint its origin to a precise moment in time. Tradition tells us that in the year 2737 BC, Emperor Shen Nong, reputedly a very learned man who was interested in the nature of life, the universe, and the way of the gods, discovered the drink in a fortuitous moment when the universe divulges one of its secrets.[4]

The Emperor Shen Nong was essentially a man of science before such a discipline had been invented. As such, his discovery of tea may have been one of the first "Eureka!" moments in human history.

Shen Nong was also known as the Yan Emperor, or the Divine Farmer. He was regarded as one of the Three August Ones of deep antiquity, along with Sui Ren Shi, who invented fire and cooking, and Fu Xi Shi, who invented fishing, hunting, and animal husbandry.

Interestingly, these three, along with several others, were collectively known as the Three Sovereigns and Five Emperors. They became rooted in Chinese history and were considered to be actual historical personalities right up until the 1920s, when a group of Chinese scholars known as the *Yigupai,* or the Doubting Antiquity School, began to question the historical record of the ancient emperors and suggested that their origin was more mythological than historical.

Whether real or imaginary, these men belong to China's rich cultural history. Shen Nong, supposedly the second of the emperors of the San Huang Period (3000–2700 BC) was regarded as the father of agriculture and of medicine. He is alleged to have tested hundreds of herbs to determine their possible medicinal effect. One of his special gifts was a sort of x-ray vision, which enabled him to see inside his body to ascertain the effects of the herbs on his organs.

Shen Nong is said to have tested hundreds of herbs and discovered many that had useful functions as medicines. In 273 BC, supposedly some two thousand years after his death, 70 of these medicinal herbs were written down in one of the classics of Chinese Medicine, *The Shen Nong pen tsao*, or *The Divine Farmer's Herb-Root Classic.* This book contained information on 365 different herbal remedies, including tea, and would become the basis of herbal medicine for two millennia.

In order to counter and prevent disease, Shen Nong apparently ordered that all water should be boiled before it was drunk—a remarkably astute precaution that is actually thought to have been responsible for preventing many of the epidemics that ravaged other civilizations. The legend goes that one day he and his entourage were visiting a distant part of his realm and they stopped to rest and partake of food and water. The emperor was sitting by a fire, over which a pot had been placed to boil water. The hot air from the fire lifted the dried leaves from the twigs of a nearby bush so that they rose and then fell into the boiling water where they infused. The smell was pleasing, and Shen Nong drank the liquid and enjoyed its taste. But most importantly, he proclaimed that it was an important medicine capable of being an antidote for seventy different poisonous herbs, as well as having a role in the treatment of many ailments. This wonderful herb was the tea plant, later named *Camellia sinensis.*

In the edition of his book produced in the seventh century, Sheng wrote that tea was beneficial for:

tumours or abscesses that come about the head, or for ailments of the bladder. It dissipates heat caused by Phlegms, or inflammations of the chest. It quenches the thirst, lessens the desire for sleep. It gladdens and cheers the heart.

An Alternate Origin

India is another of the great tea-producing and tea-drinking nations of the world, so it is not surprising to discover that it too, stakes a claim to have originated the drink.

According to Indian legend, Bodhidharma was the third son of a Tamil Pallava king from Kanchipuram. He lived in the mid-fifth century and became a Buddhist monk in the Mahayana tradition. He traveled from India to Sumatra, then to Malaya, Thailand, and China. As he went from country to country, he taught Buddhism and instructed his followers in the martial arts.

It is said that in the fifth year of a seven-year period of "wall-gazing," which he used as a meditative means of contemplating the Buddha, he began to feel drowsy and actually fell asleep. When he awoke, he was so angry with himself that he cut off his own eyelids and cast them away. A bush with curious eyelid-shaped leaves grew where they landed. Thus the tea bush was born.[5]

Another version of the tale states that as Bodhidharma felt drowsy, in order to prevent himself from closing his eyes he plucked some leaves from a nearby bush and chewed them. Immediately, he felt revived. He then gifted tea to the Buddhist world as a great aid to both meditation and spiritual development.

Bodhidharma is regarded as the person who introduced Zen Buddhism from India to China and is credited as the founder of the Shaolin school of Chinese martial arts and one of the patrons of tea.

The Evolution of Tea

Despite various myths and legends about the origin of tea, China is the likeliest birthplace of tea drinking since it was actually referred to in Chinese literature as far back as 222 AD, when it was advocated as a preferable drink to wine. It is also recorded that tea plants were cultivated in monasteries in Sichuan. A dictionary from the mid-fourth century refers to the drink as *ch'a*.

Gradually over the next two to three hundred years, tea drinking spread throughout China. While it was originally considered primarily medicinal, it came to be regarded as a pleasant and refreshing drink. Yet, the way that it was prepared underwent three distinct phases, each mirroring one of the major dynasties. Okakaru Kakuzo refers to these three phases in *The Book of Tea*, written in 1906, as the Classic, the Romantic, and the Naturalistic schools of tea.

Cake or Brick Tea

The Tang dynasty (618–907) was a period of great prosperity in China's history. Economy, politics, military power, and culture all reached great heights. A hierarchical civil service of great complexity and an educational system enabled anyone to gain high office through education and scholarship and industry. This was the time of Judge Dee and a glorious time to drink tea.

From the times of the legendary Shen Nong, tea was made by boiling fresh, unprocessed leaves. The brew would have been extremely bitter, and one can see why it would have tasted like a medicine rather than a refreshing drink. Doubtless it was an acquired taste, but to make it more palatable, people would boil it with ginger, orange peel, spices, rice, milk, or even onions. It was likely more of a soup than a cuppa.

During that time, a form of processing the tea involved drying the leaves and crushing them up before boiling. By the middle of the Tang dynasty processing reached a new level of sophistication—the tea brick.[6]

The freshly picked leaves were steamed, then dried, ground, and compressed in a flat cake or a brick mold to produce a tea cake or a tea brick. The Chinese would make these with whole, shredded, or ground leaves. Sometimes a binding agent in the form of flour, animal manure, or even animal blood would be used. The tea would then be left to dry so that it could be stacked and used as a form of currency in trade. Often, an imprint of a company or of a factory's location would be made on them.

To use the tea bricks, a piece was broken off and then toasted over a fire. This would be done to get rid of any fungus that might have grown on the brick, but also to impart a specific flavor to the tea. It would then be broken up and boiled to make drinkable tea.

Powdered Tea

The Song dynasty (960–1279) also saw great changes in its society. Whereas the Tang dynasty had used coin and commodities as currency, the Song dynasty began to use paper money. They also developed that wonder of their age: gunpowder. This dynasty also saw a significant increase in the transmission of knowledge through their invention of woodblock printing and then by movable type printing in the eleventh century.

During the Song dynasty, the Chinese developed the use of powdered tea, which was not boiled, but was rather added to already boiled water and then whisked together.

Tea drinking became more than just a pleasant beverage; drinking tea, at this time, was developed into an art form. One emperor of the Song dynasty considered drinking tea so important a process and the quality of the tea a thing of such value that he introduced the custom of bestowing gifts of tea as rewards for those individuals who were considered worthy subjects. Of course, that alone meant that people desired to have this wonderful drink, since in a way it helped to demonstrate their worthiness in society.

A poet of the Song dynasty by the name of Lichilai declared that there were three things that were most deplorable in the world. First was the

spoiling of fine youths through false education. Second was the degradation of fine art through vulgar admiration. And third was the utter waste
of fine tea through incompetent manipulation.

Steeped Tea

The great Ming dynasty (1368–1644) is considered famous for the
cultural changes that took place during that time, with advances made in
literature, science, art, and architecture. It was also during this time that
the Forbidden City in Beijing was built, as was the majority of the Great
Wall of China.

It was also during the Ming dynasty that the now popular method
of making tea was developed: the steeping of tea leaves in freshly boiled
water. This was the method that European merchants saw being used
and, inevitably, was the method that they advised to brew tea when they
started spreading it to the rest of the world.

Three Roads from China

The Tang dynasty was the period when China actively began trading with
countries beyond its borders and two great trade routes were established.
These were the Silk Road, which linked China with Asia, the Middle East,
and the Mediterranean; and the Tea-Horse Road, which linked China
with Tibet and Burma.

The Silk Road was not actually a single route but rather a network of
routes that camel caravans trudged along, crossing India, Persia, parts of
Africa, and finally to the Mediterranean and Europe.[7] Merchants traded
Chinese silk and tea bricks in exchange for spices and much needed
horses.

Similarly, merchants on the Tea-Horse Road, which was also known
as the Southern Silk Road, traded tea for hardy Tibetan horses.[8]

Centuries later, once China had begun trade with Russia, the Tea
Road—also known as the Siberian Route—was established. The main
trade was tea for Siberian furs. The countries along the various roads
adopted tea drinking, each developing their own style of tea beverage.

To Japan, the Land of the Rising Sun

In the sixth century, Buddhist monks from China traveled to Japan, bringing along with them their tea habit. To feed and nurture that habit they also brought tea plants, although tea drinking did not gain popular approval immediately in Japan.

Then, in 1191, a Zen Buddhist priest by the name of Eisai (1141–1215) returned to Japan from China and established the Rinzai sect of Zen Buddhism. He brought with him tea seeds and powdered tea. The seeds were grown and established at a temple near Kyoto. As a result, Eisai became known as the "Father of Tea" in Japan. Tea enjoyed an elevated status in Zen Buddhism, for it was found to be a useful aid to ward off sleepiness and to improve concentration during meditation.

During the Muromachi period (1336–1573), when Japan was ruled by the shoguns of the Ashikaga clan, a tea cult based on aesthetics came into being. The cult was based upon the ritual way of making tea in China, using special utensils and implements. Gradually, the manner of preparation of the drink became ever more ritualized by several tea masters as part of Zen practice. The first of these was the fifteenth-century monk Murata Shuko (1422–1502), who is credited as the founder of the Japanese tea ceremony, which is called *chanoyu*.

Shuko was an aesthetic adviser to the shogun Ashikaga Yoshimasa. He advocated carrying out the whole ceremony in a small teahouse built for the purpose with a floor space of four-and-a-half *tatami* mats. The room was to be furnished simply with shelves for artwork and plain walls for Zen calligraphy. The actual tea making followed a set ritual.

The next great tea master of note was Sen no Rikyu (1522–1591), who refined and perfected the tea ceremony. He laid down a precise order for performing the various elements, using particular utensils. He took the Shuko's teahouse design and modified it, making it smaller so that it had a floor space of only two *tatami* mats.† The entrance was to be through a

---

† A *tatami* mat is a traditional Japanese floor covering made of rice straw. The mat is oblong with the ratio of length:width of exactly 2:1. Sizes vary according to region, but generally a tatami mat is 1.91 m x .995 m.

small door, and the whole teahouse was to be secluded in a Zen garden. It was essentially only large enough for sitting and having tea.

Rikyu also established the concepts of *wabi*, or deliberate simplicity in life, and of *sabi*, meaning appreciation of the faded and old. He is also credited with creating the idea of *wabi-cha*—the approach to the tea ceremony. This consisted of the four expressions: *wa*, meaning harmony, *kei*, meaning respect, *sei*, meaning purity, and *jaku*, meaning calmness and tranquility.

This did not mean, however, that the tea ceremony was an insipid affair or only a practice for people given over solely to art and intellectual pursuits. The tea ceremony was part and parcel of the way of the samurai. On the one hand, samurai understood and practiced the arts of fighting in the *budo* in preparation for the battlefield; yet in the teahouse, they practiced *chanoyu*, the tea ceremony, and learned *chado*, the way of tea, which would help discipline the mind and give inner understanding and strength.

Although the origins were very much based in Zen teaching, in time *chado* developed just as strong of a tradition in secular life as with the monks. In Japan, the tearoom, or *cha-shitsu*, may be a special room in the home that one enters on his or her knees. We shall return to this in chapter 10.

Chapter Three

Tea Classics of Literature

Tea is nought but this:
First you heat the water,
Then you make the tea.
Then you drink it properly.
That is all you need to know.

      Sen no Rikyu (1522–1591), Zen Tea Master

Tea . . . is a religion of the art of life.

      Kakuzō Okakura (1862–1913), The Book of Tea

UNSURPRISINGLY, TEA, AS THE SECOND-MOST COMMON drink after water, has accumulated an extensive literature.

China

The very first reference to tea was in 222 AD, in an obscure piece of Chinese writing mentioning the beverage as a good substitute for wine. Then, in the third century, in a dictionary called the *Kuang Ya* written by Zhang Yi, a scholar who held the rank of Doctor of the Imperial Academy, the first written description of how to make tea is given:

> The cakes [of tea] were roasted until reddish brown in color, pounded into tiny pieces, and placed in a chinaware pot. Boiling water was then poured over them, after which onion, ginger, and orange were added.

Tea doesn't sound to have been terribly palatable in this first reference—more of a soup than a drink. Indeed, for the first few centuries of its existence, tea was treated more as a medicine than a refreshing beverage.

By the time of the Tang dynasty (618–907), tea had become an accompaniment to intellectual pursuits. Drinking tea had become a sophisticated event, something people did while pondering beauty, while philosophizing on the wonders of the universe, or while writing poetry.

There are, in fact, over one hundred Chinese monographs about tea from the Tang dynasty to the Ming dynasty.

Taoism—the Way

Taoism is about the Tao.[9] This is usually translated as "the Way." But it is hard to say exactly what Tao means. Tao is the ultimate creative principle of the universe. All things are unified and connected in the Tao. It originated in China about two thousand years ago and is essentially a religion of unity and opposites: yin and yang.

The principle of yin and yang sees the world as filled with complementary forces—action and non-action; light and dark; hot and cold; and so on. Taoism aims to achieve harmony or union with the universe and with nature through self-development. Taoist practices include meditation, feng shui, and fortune-telling. The preparation and drinking of tea developed into a ritual under the influence of Taoism in ancient China.

Lao Tse, a sixth century philosopher and supposed keeper of records at the imperial court, wrote the book *Tao Te Ching*, which can be translated as *The Law of Virtue and Its Way*. He is regarded by many as the father of Taoism. His book is certainly one of the most influential in history.

The Classic of Tea 茶经

This is *the* classic about tea. It was written by Lu Yu sometime between 760 and 780.[10] The book is not a huge tome by Chinese standards, but it is written in the poetic scholarly style of the Tang dynasty. It consists of three scrolls, or three volumes, containing ten chapters in total. After the Tang dynasty, the three volumes were bound into a single book.[11]

Lu Yu (733–804) is respected and venerated as the sage of tea. He was born in Tianmen, a city in the central Hubei province. He was an orphan and was adopted by a Buddhist monk of the Dragon Cloud monastery. The life of a monk did not suit him though, so he ran away, joined a circus, and became a clown.

This carefree existence was not to last, and in his teen years, he was apprenticed to Master Zou Fouzi in the mountain monastery of Houmen. There he learned about herbs and medicines and studied tea. He became adept in preparing tea for his master and fellow apprentices. It is reported that one day while out searching for tea plants and other herbs, he stumbled upon a spring. He brewed some tea using the water and was amazed at how good it tasted. This convinced him that tea as a drink depended upon the quality of the water used, and he was not wrong.

After six years of study, he left the monastery and devoted himself to writing. He lived with other artists and scholars and began to write the *Ch'a Ching*, or *The Classic of Tea*. This book covers every aspect of tea, including the way it should be grown and harvested, the tools needed to prepare it as a drink, and the ways in which it should be drunk.

Lu Yu starts by describing the legendary beginnings of tea, then he goes on to describe the ancient giant tea tree in the Bashan Xiachuan area. He talks about the plant's structure, its growing characteristics, and the sort of soil that it needs. He gives an almost scientific description of the botanical features and the correct way to cultivate it to get the best quality tea. He outlines the tools used to cultivate, harvest, and process tea and describes the right time of day, the season, and the climate needed for plucking the leaves. Lastly, he describes the technique of making tea bricks, meticulously describing all the tools used in the process.

Drinking tea is a serious affair in Lu Yu's opinion, and he explains the various methods of drinking tea. He even gives a beautiful description of how the water should be boiled:

> When the water is boiling—it must look like fishes' eyes and give off but the hint of a sound. When at the edges it chatters like a bubbling spring and looks like pearls innumerable strung together, it has reached the second stage. When it leaps like breakers majestic and resounds like a swelling wave, it is at its peak. Any more and the water will be boiled out and should not be used.

After all that, Lu Yu discusses the health benefits of tea as well as the use of tea in cooking and in tea recipes. All in all, the book truly deserves its title.

Report on Brewing Tea 煎茶水记

This is another tea classic that was written in 814 by Zhang Youxin. It is a monograph devoted entirely to boiling water for use with tea leaves.

Youxin describes using water from seven sources, with such delightful names as Suzhou Tiger Hill Temple Spring and Temple of Small Gods Fountain. He describes the quality of the water and its value in making tea. These water sources are all especially good and far better than the water from twenty other less fortunate areas that he describes.

The Treatise on Tea 大观茶论

In 1107, Emperor Huizong of the Song dynasty wrote a quite amazing book that ranks second to Lu Yu's book in the Chinese classics about tea. In *The Treatise on Tea*, Emperor Huizong describes the Song way of taking tea and lists all the qualities of tea and its preparation, as well as illustrates how to be discriminating in tasting tea.

Pictorial of Tea Ware 茶具图赞

Pictorial of Tea Ware is an illustrated book written in 1269 during the Song dynasty by "Old Man Shenan."[12] It describes the whisking method of preparing tea from tea cake to finished drink. This whisking method resulted in foam being produced. This was subsequently superseded by the brewing method in China, but it actually spread to Japan, where it became the basis for the way that tea is made in Japan to this day. As we shall see in chapter 10, it is the essence of the famous Japanese tea ceremony.

The Song of Tea, *or* The Seven Bowls of Tea 七碗诗 卢仝

The Song of Tea is a poem by Lu Tung (790–835), a Chinese poet of the Tang dynasty who devoted his life to tea, the tea ceremony, and poetry. Apparently, tea was more important to him that anything else, even his own legacy as a poet. He once said, "I am not interested in immortality but only in tea flavor."

Lu Tung was a Taoist recluse who was born into an aristocratic family. He was destined for officialdom but dropped out to became something of a dilettante before opting for Taoist study and the life of an ascetic. His poetry was much admired at court for it was considered intense and scholarly. His poem *The Song of Tea*, otherwise known as *The Seven Bowls of Tea*, comes from his book *Writing Thanks to Imperial Grand Master of Remonstrance Meng for Sending New Tea*. The poem would become as famous as Lu Yu's *Cha Ching*. Following is an excerpt from the poem:

The first bowl moistens my lips and throat.
The second bowl breaks my loneliness.
The third bowl searches my barren entrail,
but to find therein some thousand volumes of odd ideographs.
The fourth bowl raises a slight perspiration;
all the wrongs of life pass out through my pores.

At the fifth bowl I am purified.
The sixth bowl calls me to the realms of the immortals.
The seventh bowl—ah, but I could take no more!
I only feel the breath of the cool wind that rises in my sleeves.
Where is Paradise? Let me ride on this sweet breeze and waft away
　　thither.

Lu Tong met his end during the infamous Ganlu Incident, when Emperor Wenzong attempted to wrestle power from the eunuchs. Lu Tong, at the wrong place at the wrong time, was accused of treason. He was imprisoned, tried, and executed, apparently with a nail to the back of his head.

Japan

Japan also has its classics of tea literature. This was inevitable, giving the direction that tea drinking took in Japan, where it became elevated to a philosophy. The Way of Tea, or the Japanese tea ceremony, became a ritualized rite that was, and still is, practiced widely throughout Japan.

Southern Record　南方録

Southern Record is a book about the teachings of Sen no Rikyu, the tea saint. The original book was lost for over a hundred years, so this version, which has been in circulation for a long time, may not contain all of the original teachings.

Sen no Rikyu (1522–1591) was a tea master who was instrumental in developing the tea ceremony in Japan. Nanbo Sokei, a Zen priest and disciple of Rikyu, wrote the original *Southern Record*, but after Rikyu's death, both the book and Sokei disappeared.

A century later, in 1688, it was rediscovered and transcribed by Tachibana Jitsuzan. He produced a five-volume work, which he extended to seven after further fragments of the original were discovered. Tea scholars, to this day, still dispute its authenticity.

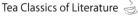

Treatise on Tea Drinking for Health 喫茶養生記

Written in 1193 by the Zen Buddhist monk Myoan Eisai (1141–1215), this is the oldest Japanese classic on tea. Eisai brought green tea from China to Japan, and he is the first Japanese person to write about using tea for religious rather than health purposes.

The Book of Tea

The Book of Tea is a slim volume written in 1911 by Kakuzo Okakura. It was originally written in English and is considered a modern treatise on the tea ceremony written by a Japanese citizen who had received a Western education. It provides an interesting examination of the Western view of Japan and its tea culture. It looks at the aesthetics of tea, which Okakura deems "teaism."

For anyone wanting to study this aspect of tea, Okakura's book is the first to read. He discussed Zen and the way that tea has weaved its way into ordinary Japanese life. Okakura further emphasizes how Japanese ideas of simplicity have had a profound effect on art, architecture, and an entire way of life. Teaism is about practicing humanity and helping the individual to discipline the mind through the ritual of preparing and drinking tea.

Chapter Four

The Tea Trade

Some people will tell you there is a great deal of poetry and fine sentiment in a chest of tea.

Ralph Waldo Emerson (1803–182), Letters and Social Aims

Tea Travels to Europe

NOWADAYS, IT SEEMS STRANGE TO THINK THAT WHILE tea has been consumed for so long in China and Asia, its introduction to Europe did not take place until the sixteenth century. Tea came to Europe along the Silk Road, that ancient trade channel between the civilizations of antiquity. Although it was regarded as an herb, it was not until 1559 that we find any written record of it being used as a drink on the European continent. The Venetian writer Giovanni Battista Ramusio recounts in his book, *Navigatione et Viaggi*, that he had been told about "chai catai," a medicinal drink:

> They take of that herb, whether dry or fresh, and boil it well in water. One or two cups of this decoction taken on an empty stomach removes fever, headache, stomach-ache, pain in the side or in the joints, and it should be taken as hot as you can bear it.

Further, the Portuguese had gained trading rights in Macao in 1535. In 1557, they established a colony there and established trade routes to

India, Japan, and China. Whereas Giovanni Battista Ramusio was the first European to write about tea, the first European to actually taste it was the Portuguese Jesuit priest Father Jasper de Cruz. While he was staying in China in 1560, he wrote a letter home to Portugal relating how he had sampled tea and thought it delicious.

Soon after, the Portuguese began shipping tea to Lisbon and, since Portugal had a trade agreement with Holland, the Dutch East India Company started shipping cargoes of tea back to Holland, France, and the Baltic region.

However, in 1602, relations became frosty between Holland and Portugal when the Dutch East India Company and the Dutch West India Company began invading Portuguese colonies in the Americas, Africa, and Asia. This was the start of the Dutch-Portuguese War, which would drag on for sixty-one years. With the end of the agreement between the two countries, the Dutch East India Company took control of the entire tea trade to the West.

The East India Companies

There were several East India Companies formed across continental Europe during the seventeenth century, each chartered to trade with countries in Asia. The oldest was the East India Company, which was granted a Royal Charter by Queen Elizabeth I of England in 1600. This charter gave the company a monopoly on trade with all countries east of the Cape of Good Hope and west of the Straits of Magellan.

The Dutch East India Company, established in 1602, secured a twenty-one-year monopoly from the States-General of the Netherlands to trade in Asia. This company grew quickly and soon dominated trade, thanks in no small measure to its highly efficient army and navy. The Portuguese East India Company followed in 1616, then the French East India Company in 1664, and finally the Swedish East India Company in 1731.

The East India Company was moderately successful and had established good relationships with the Chinese court and also with Japan by

1619. (This was thanks to having joined forces with the Dutch East India Company to engage with and blow Spanish and Portuguese ships out of the waters around the coast of China.) It was not long, however, before the English and the Dutch began hostilities, leading to the first Anglo-Dutch War (1652–1656). The English won the war, and the Dutch had to accept that the British would hold the monopoly on trade with all the English-speaking colonies.

The second Anglo-Dutch war occurred between 1665–1667, and this time the Dutch were victorious. Again, the spoils of war were the precious trades in tea and spices. There would be two other such wars between the two nations, from 1672–1674 and again from 1780–1784. The latter was related to the American War of Independence, which we shall consider in chapter 5. Suffice it to say that the Dutch won in the end, and the East India Company effectively withdrew from the China seas to concentrate on trade with India. This would actually prove to be a fortuitous move for the East India Company once tea growth had become established in India in the early nineteenth century.

Tea to Russia

In 1638, Tsar Michel I was given a consignment of four *poods* of tea by a Mongolian ruler.[13] A *pood* was a Russian measure of weight, roughly equivalent to thirty-five pounds (16 kilograms). The tsar was delighted and wanted more tea. As a result, diplomacy reached a new level and tea was very much put on the agenda.

In 1679, China and Russia agreed to a trade treaty, which saw a regular trade by camel caravan between the two nations. Chinese tea was traded for Russian furs along this route. It was a difficult trade route, however, so the cost of tea became extremely high and only the Russian royalty and nobility could afford it. Then, in 1689, the Treaty of Nerchinsk, which gave Russia sovereignty over Siberia, was followed by the establishment of the Tea Road from China through Siberia and into Russia.

Catherine the Great increased tea imports along the Tea Road, and by the time of her death in 1796, Russia was importing three million pounds (a little over one million kilograms) of tea each year—in the form of loose tea and tea bricks—by camel caravan. The amount of tea imported, however, was enough to considerably drop the price and so tea finally became available to the Russian middle and lower classes.

Tea in America

Back in the mid-seventeenth century, New York was still a Dutch settlement called New Amsterdam. The director-general of the colony was an interesting man named Peter Stuyvesant. He had joined the Dutch West India Company in 1635, and became the director of the company's colony of Curacao in 1642. Two years later, he led an attack against the Spanish island of Saint Martin and was struck by a cannonball, resulting in him having to have an amputation and be fitted with a wooden leg reinforced with silver bands, which gave rise to his nickname of "Old Silver Leg."

Stuyvesant was not a tolerant man by all accounts, as evidenced by him ordering the public torture of a young Quaker preacher and by his refusal to permit Jews from Northern Brazil to settle in New Amsterdam. The latter was a decision that he was later forced to rescind under public pressure.

Around 1650, when he became the director-general of New Amsterdam, Stuyvesant famously introduced tea to the colony. The drink became immensely popular, and by the end of the century (by which time the settlement had been renamed as New York), more tea was being drunk in the colony than was being drunk in the whole of England.

Tea to England

The first tea shipments to arrive in England came in 1657, as a consignment traded with the Dutch East India Company. Yet it was not until 1662 that tea started to become a sensation in the country, and this was due to the forthcoming marriage of King Charles II to Catherine of Braganza, the daughter of King Juan IV of Portugal. The good lady had been betrothed to King Charles II, who had been restored to the throne in 1660, after the death of Oliver Cromwell in 1658.

The marriage contract resulted in England gaining Tangier in North Africa and the city of Bombay (modern Mumbai) in India, along with trading rights in Brazil and the East Indies.

When Catherine arrived in England, she brought with her a chest of tea. She was a devotee of tea, which by then was the favored drink of the Portuguese nobility. Not surprisingly, once she had become queen, her partiality for tea established a fashion in England, and soon all of the ladies at court were sipping it.

Despite its popularity at court and in affluent society, tea was not a drink for the common English folk until much later as it was expensive. In 1664, the East India Company started to import Chinese tea from Java, which began with a presentation of a few pounds of tea to King Charles, to curry favor with him, so that he could keep in Catherine's good favor. The king liked the tea, and in 1669, all Dutch imports were banned, and the East India Company held a monopoly over the country's trade. Gradually, over the next thirty years, tea imports increased until the drink became cheap enough for it to be available for mass consumption by all English citizens.

The diarist Samuel Pepys, who recounts 1660s London, gives us a fascinating insight into life during the Restoration.[14] He provides eyewitness accounts of the Great Plague of London (1665–1666) and the Great Fire of London (1666). But it is his vignettes and snippets about daily life that are so enchanting, such as his entry for September 25, 1660:

To the office, where Sir W. Batten, Collonell Slingsby, and I sat awhile; and Sir R. Ford coming to us about some business, we talked together of the interest of this kingdom to have a peace with Spain and a War with France and Holland—where Sir R. Ford talked like a man of great reason and experience. And afterwards did send for a cupp of tee (a China drink of which I never had drank before) and went away.

By the mid-eighteenth century, some six million pounds (nearly three million kilograms) of tea were being exported from China to England. This compared with 4.5 million (2 million kg) being carried by Dutch boats and a mere 2 million (900,000 kg) by French traders.

The Tea Clippers

During the nineteenth century, the need for tea was so great around the globe that the tea trade necessitated slick transportation. This meant that ships used for trading had to be as fast as possible. Thus began the era of the clippers.[15]

These great sailing ships had three masts and a square rig. They were narrow, very tall, and as fast as shipbuilders could make at that time. Clippers sailed all over the world, carrying spices, tea, tobacco, and opium, of which we shall read about later in chapter 5. These ships clipped over the waves—meaning that they sailed swiftly over the waves instead of lumbering through them like prior heavier vessels.

All the Way from China

During the time of the East India Company, tea crops were grown almost exclusively by Chinese farmers who had two pickings a year—in April and June—in order to sell and export their goods. They also aimed for two additional pickings in late summer for home use. [16]

Tea buyers would pack the tea into a "chop" consisting of around six hundred tea chests. These would then be transported by "coolies" across the mountains to the nearest tea center where buyers would select their goods. Then barges transported the chops by canal to the ports, where a second selection took place by the buyers of the various East India Companies. It was an arduous journey fraught with potential danger to the tea, which was vulnerable to rain and inclement weather, as well as to the transporters, who were prey to gangs of robbers. In all, it could take six to eight weeks for tea to come from bush to port.

After arriving in port, a long trip by sea ensued, and the race to get the tea to the market in Paris and London was on. By the time tea was sold as "fresh tea," the leaves were usually about eighteen months old.

In London, the East India Company established its base on Mincing Lane. This would become the center of the tea and spice trade for many years to come. Not unsurprisingly, it would also become the center of the opium trade since the three commodities were linked and lead to the murky dealings that would result in the Opium Wars in the nineteenth century.

Tea to India

The story of the introduction of tea to India revolves around an interesting Scottish Victorian explorer named Robert Fortune (1812–1880).[17] Robert came from humble origins and rose to become one of the most important and influential plant discoverers of his age. He was born in Berwickshire, Scotland. After school, he obtained an apprenticeship as a nurseryman in a local garden and very quickly demonstrated an aptitude for botany. As a result, he secured employment at the Edinburgh Botanic Garden in 1840. From there, in 1842, he took up an appointment in the Hothouse Department at the Horticultural Society's Garden in London. Fortune smiled on Fortune, and he was eventually given the post of the Horticultural Society's Collector in China.

In 1843, after taking a slow boat to Hong Kong, Fortune set about searching for a number of plants that he had been requested to bring back to England. Among these were blue-flowered peonies, various orchids, giant peaches said to grow in the emperor's garden, and tea. Armed with many of the newly invented Wardian cases—small portable greenhouses of various shapes and designs that prevented plants from drying out—he went off in pursuit of his quarry.

Over the next three years, Fortune made several clandestine excursions into the northern provinces of China. He was the archetypal intrepid explorer, braving fevers, angry xenophobic mobs (since the first opium war had only ended in 1842), storms on the Yellow Sea, and pirates on the Yangtze River.

Rather like a latter day Indiana Jones, Fortune steeped himself in the Chinese culture, learned Mandarin, and took to wearing disguises so that he would better blend in with the locals. He even shaved his head, then grew a pigtail, and donned Chinese clothes. He was not averse to fighting when needed and used a fowling gun to scare off pirates who attacked him on one of his visits. Upon returning to London in 1846, Fortune wrote a book based on his journals entitled *Three Years' Wanderings in the Northern Provinces of China.*

Fortune returned to China in 1848, on behalf of the East India Company with the mission to seek out and obtain the finest tea plants in order to establish tea plantations in India. He had to travel far into the mountainous areas, well beyond the range permitted by the local authorities. Nonetheless, Fortune and his team of workers managed to transport some twenty thousand plants and seedlings in Wardian cases to the Himalayas. He also brought with him Chinese tea workers skilled in the methods of preparing tea in order to establish the method in the new Indian plantations in Darjeeling.

Yet Fortune was not merely an adventurer. He made very important discoveries and introduced over 120 different species of plants to the gardens of the West. Some of them would be named after him. He was also the first European to discover that black and green tea came from the same tree.

Tea to the Rest of the World

By the end of the nineteenth century, tea growing was spreading all over the globe to places wherever tea plants could be sustained. Tea plantations were established in Ceylon (now Sri Lanka), Korea, Formosa, Sumatra, Russian Georgia, Natal, Malawi, Uganda, Kenya, Congo, Tanzania, Mozambique, Brazil, Argentina, Peru, and also in Australia. Surprisingly, tea plantations can now be found in England and Wales.

Chapter Five

Tempests in Teapots

So inscrutable is the arrangement of causes and consequences in this world, that a two-penny duty on tea, unjustly imposed in a sequestered part of it, changes the condition of all its inhabitants.

Thomas Jefferson (1743–1826), Autobiography of Thomas Jefferson

FOR A DRINK THAT IS ASSOCIATED WITH CALMNESS, peace, and tranquility, tea has stirred up a lot of trouble over the years. What may have seemed like storms in teacups escalated into major tempests in teapots.

TEMPEST IN A TEAPOT

There are a number of idioms used around the world that convey a small event that gets blown out of proportion.

Idioms are interesting since they are used in virtually every culture. They are figures of expression that we use to illustrate something. People like to use them and consider them to be normal speech. It is estimated that there are around twenty-five thousand of them littering the English language.

Idioms are not to be taken literally. After all, you do not actually get tempests in teapots, or storms in teacups, as the British tend to say.

The concept of a tempest in a teapot is archaic, predating the use of tea in our culture. Marcus Tullius Cicero (106–43 BC), the great Roman philosopher, lawyer, and orator, used a similar idiom: *Gratidius excitabat fluctus in simpulo, ut dicatur* which means, "Gratidius has raised a tempest in a ladle, as the saying goes."

But it was Lord North, the British prime minister during the reign of King George III, who coined the term in relation to the American colonists' outrage over the tax on tea.

Other languages also use the expression. The Chinese use the phrases:

茶杯裡的風波 which means storm in a teacup

or

茶壺裡的風暴 which means tempest in a teapot

A Colonial Drink

It was inevitable that the fledgling colonies in America should be tea drinkers, considering that many of the early settlers were from Britain, Holland, and Portugal—all countries where tea drinking had become well established.

William Penn, the founder of the Quaker city of Philadelphia, was a great advocate of tea, which he felt gladdened the spirits, but did not have the inebriating effects as that demon of all drinks: alcohol.

George Washington was also a confirmed tea drinker according to his step-granddaughter, Nellie; his habitual breakfast consisted of three cups of tea and three or four pancakes made from cornmeal, which he ate with butter and honey.

During the time of the American colonies, things were pretty dire in England, for the Seven Year's War, which had raged from 1756 to 1763, had drained the coffers of the British Empire. In an attempt to raise revenue, the British government decided to levy taxes on their American colonies. In 1764, the Sugar Act was passed, followed by the Stamp Act in 1765. The latter required printed materials in the colony to be produced on specially stamped paper from London, on which a revenue stamp was embossed. It was hugely unpopular in the colonies and was repealed the following year. Soon after, Charles Townshend, the British Chancellor of the Exchequer, entered the scene. By all accounts, Townshend was a witty orator and a wily politician. He came up with the idea that some £40,000 could be generated by taxing the colonies on the importation of several commodities, including lead, paper, glass, and tea. Beginning in 1767, Townshend passed several resolutions through parliament, which came to be known as the Townshend Acts.[18] Understandably, these caused great disgruntlement in the colonies, tensions soared, and the colonies finally resisted the taxes.

At that time, the East India Company had a monopoly on the tea trade with the colonies, which had previously been circumvented by the development of a black market fed by tea smuggled directly from Holland. The first Townshend Act cracked down on smuggling as well, bringing the monopoly back to the East India Company.

However, parliament submitted to pressure at the outcry caused by the act and repealed it in 1767. The tensions that had been created were worsened in 1768, however, when British troops were garrisoned in Boston, Massachusetts, in order to protect the British officials who were attempting to enforce the legislation. In 1770, a mob formed around a British sentry, verbally abusing the man. Eight other British soldiers arrived to support him. Objects were thrown at the group, and the soldiers lost their self-control. Without orders, they fired into the crowd, killing three people instantly and injuring several others. Two of the wounded died some days later.

The crowd eventually dispersed after the governor promised an official inquiry into the tragedy, but the following day another mob formed, which prompted the British troops to withdraw to the safety of Fort Independence on Castle Island. Subsequently, eight soldiers, one officer, and three civilians were arrested and tried for murder. The twelve people were defended by John Adams, who would become the second president of the United States in 1797. He secured the acquittal of six of the soldiers and the reduced conviction of two on the charge of manslaughter. Their punishment was to be branded on the hand.

The British attempted to minimize the event by referring to it as "the incident on King Street," while the colonists called it "the Boston Massacre." The silversmith Paul Revere prepared an engraving of the event from an earlier engraving by Henry Pelham, and its rapid distribution served to keep tempers simmering.

That year, most of the Townshend Acts were repealed, except for the one about tea. This led people in the colonies to stop drinking imported tea; as a substitute, they began drinking "liberty tea," which was essentially herbal tea. The decline in the amount of tea being imbibed by the colonists meant that the East India Company were left with a huge surplus of tea, and since it was already in debt to the government, the company faced bankruptcy.

In 1773, Lord North's government passed the Tea Act, which gave the East India Company sole right to trade tea to America and to sell it to tea merchants without paying any duty. This was effectively a means of bailing out the East India Company since it was not expected to pay duty; yet the colonies were still expected to pay the Townshend tax on the tea.

The company duly sent sixty thousand tons of tea on seven ships to ports in Boston, New York, Charleston, and Philadelphia. The ships to New York and Philadelphia were not permitted to dock and were sent back with their cargo of tea. In Charleston, the ship's crew unloaded its tea, but the leaves were left to rot on the dock. In Boston, the ships were allowed to dock and unload all cargo, except for the tea. This created a problem, since the ships were under orders not to return to Britain without having discharged of their tea cargo. It was an impasse, which lasted until the December 16, 1773, the date on which the Townshend tax was to be paid.

That night, colonists, disguised as Indians, boarded the three ships and dumped the cargo of tea into the Boston harbor. The event went down in history as the Boston Tea Party.

George Hewes, an eyewitness to the event, wrote:

> In about three hours from the time we went on board, we had thus broken and thrown overboard every tea chest to be found on the ship, while those in the other ships were disposing of the tea in the same way, at the same time. We were surrounded by the British armed ships, but no attempt was made to resist us. . . . And it was observed at that time that the stillest night ensued that Boston had enjoyed for many months.

Lord North declared that it was merely a tempest in a teapot and expected that the distemper would settle down. It was a faint hope, which was hardly helped by the ending of self-government in Massachusetts and the imposition of British control under the command of General Thomas Gage. It was not long before the battles of Lexington and Concord were waged and the Declaration of Independence of 1776 was signed.

The Opium Wars

During the eighteenth century, the average British working family was spending about 5 percent of its food budget on tea. But tea was expensive, as it had to be brought from China and was mainly paid for with silver and with cotton from India. However, China started to produce its own cotton, with the effect that the cotton from India was not needed. The British then tried to pay for the tea with British woolen fabrics but without success, as the Chinese had a preference for silk. Thus, the East India Company began using another product from India to pay for their tea: opium from Bengal.

The East India Company owned vast opium plantations and sold opium in the auction markets in Calcutta (modern day Kolkata), in Southern India. Other British and Persian companies that traded with China at the discretion of the East India Company bought the opium. They then paid the East India Company in silver, which had been paid to them by the Chinese through an illegal opium smuggling trade. It wasn't long before about 10 percent of the Chinese population was addicted to opium. This is a particularly dark period of British imperial history, since the East India Company fostered this smuggling enterprise to get opium into China so that it could then use the Chinese silver to buy tea for its citizens.

The Emperor of China was outraged, since opium had been banned from the country by imperial edict in 1729, due to its highly addictive nature and the effect it was having on the Chinese people. The emperor sent one of his best officials, Lin Tse-hsu (1785–1850) to Canton to try to curb the situation. He studied the problem and made three proposals. First, he suggested rounding up all the addicts and breaking their opium addiction. Second, he wanted to punish the opium dealers. And finally, he proposed confiscating foreign merchants' stores of opium and threatening to punish them under Chinese law.

Despite all this, the illicit opium trade continued, with The East India Company bribing local officials to turn a blind eye to the nefarious trade. At last, in 1839, Emperor Daoguang declared a war on opium and ordered raids on foreign traders. Goods valued at £2 million were seized, including forty-two thousand opium pipes and twenty thousand chests of opium.

The British government responded by sending a fleet of sixteen warships and four thousand troops to the Pearl River Delta, near Humen. The first Opium War had begun. With their superior firepower, the British troops overwhelmed the Chinese defenses, and Chinese losses were immense—over twenty thousand fatalities, compared to a mere sixty-nine British killed. The Chinese empire had been brought to its knees, and the Treaty of Nanking was signed aboard the HMS *Cornwallis* in August 1842, bringing the war to an end.

The terms of the treaty were punitive. The British Empire was paid 21 million silver US dollars in compensation for its loss of earnings and the cost of the war. China also opened five ports for the trade of opium and, most significantly, it ceded Hong Kong to the British.

Conflict broke out again during the Second Opium War between 1856 and 1860. This time, the British were aided by the French, and once again, China was forced to sign a treaty at the Convention of Peking. The emperor had been forced to flee, so Prince Gong, his brother, signed the treaty. The opium trade was again legalized, increased trade was agreed to, and the district of Kowloon was ceded to the British. In addition, freedom of religion was established, both Britain and France received substantial financial compensation for the war, and British ships were permitted to carry indentured Chinese to America as laborers.

The Sri Lankan Conflict

Although tea was not a direct tool in the Sri Lankan conflict, it did have a part to play in the origins of this dreadful modern-day war that raged from 1983 to 2009, and which claimed the lives of over one hundred thousand people.

Sri Lanka is a teardrop-shaped island 30 miles (50 kilometers) off the southern tip of India. It has had many names over the years. Its Arabic name, used as long ago as the fourth century, was Serendip, from which we get the English word "serendipity." It became something of a pawn during the imperialist centuries, when the Dutch, the Portuguese, and ultimately the British, who called it Ceylon, claimed it as their own. The country achieved independence in 1948, and in 1972, it was renamed Sri Lanka, meaning "resplendent island." It is also known by its nickname: India's teardrop.

Sri Lanka is not a large island. It is only 215 miles (350 kilometers) long by 110 miles (180 kilometers) wide. It is a beautiful island, with central mountains ideal for growing tea, lush forests and plains, wonderful coastal beaches, and a pleasant climate. The population is twenty million, of whom the majority are Sinhalese, with many ethnic minorities including Tamils, Muslim Moors, Burghers, Kaffirs, and Malays. It is a republic governed by a presidential system.

The island is one of the world's largest tea exporters, producing 20 percent of the world's tea. Yet tea was unknown to the island until 1860. At that time, Sri Lanka was a British colony, and coffee production was one of its main exports. Then a rust fungus, *Hemileia vastratrix*, devastated the coffee plantations, and a substitute economic exporter was desperately needed.

James Taylor, a Scotsman, arrived in Ceylon in 1852. In 1867, after the collapse of the coffee crops, Taylor visited India to learn about tea production. Upon his return in 1867, he established the first tea plantation on the Loolecondera estate in Kandy. By 1872, he had added a tea factory. He was so successful that the mere twenty pounds of tea he grew when he started grew to over twenty-two thousand tons of tea by 1890.

In 1890, the Scottish millionaire Thomas Lipton, a colorful character who had been a cabin boy, grocer, bookkeeper, and door-to-door salesman in America, visited Taylor. Lipton had already established a business known as Lipton's Tea and saw the huge potential of using Ceylon tea. He entered into business dealings with Taylor and started to distribute his tea to Europe and the rest of the world. Thus, Lipton's tea empire was born.

Taylor and other British plantation owners had brought in Tamil laborers from the Southern Indian state of Tamil Nadu to work on the tea plantations, since many had experience of working on the plantations in their home state. Over the generations, the Tamil population settled and became an integral part of the island.

After Sri Lankan independence in 1948, however, religious and ethnic tension between the Tamil minority and the Singhalese majority deepened (the Tamils were predominately Hindu and the Sinhalese predominantly Buddhist). Tension gave way to armed conflict and skirmishes gave way to outright war, as the Tamils' demand for an independent state of Tamil—called Tamil Eelam—in the north and east of the island was refused by the Singhalese. The insurgents called themselves the Liberation Tigers of Tamil Eelam, or the LTTE. They also became known as the Tamil Tigers.

After twenty-six years of bloody war, including suicide bombings by Tamil Tigers, the government forces launched a major offensive, and the Tamil Tigers were finally forced to admit defeat. The Sri Lankan government claimed itself to be the first country in the world to defeat terrorism. The aftermath of the war has seen allegations of war crimes made against both sides and investigation by the United Nations was begun. Both sides strenuously denied the allegations, and the investigation is still being carried out at the time of writing this book.

Tea production was, of course, affected during the conflict, but it has been steadily increasing over the last decade. In 2008, export earnings struck a record level of $1.23 billion, which was an increase from $1.02 billion in 2007. Unfortunately, as with many industries across the world, the global financial crisis saw a 30 percent drop in overseas sales in 2009.

You Can't Blame the Tea

Although we have seen that tea has been a factor in several conflicts and issues throughout history, it is not tea itself that is to blame. Tea in those instances was simply a commodity. It has been something that people want and that they have been prepared to barter for. Yet, despite even its association with opium, tea itself remains a wholesome drink.

Chapter Six

The Smugglers

Five and twenty ponies,
Trotting through the dark—
Brandy for the Parson, 'Baccy for the Clerk.
Them that asks no questions isn't told a lie—
Watch the wall my darling while the Gentlemen go by.

Rudyard Kipling (1865–1936), "A Smuggler's Song"

B Y THE BEGINNING OF THE EIGHTEENTH CENTURY, TEA was established as a popular drink in Britain and its colonies. The problem was that tea was hugely expensive. The East India Company had a monopoly on its trade, and it felt no compunction to lower its price. Indeed, the East India Company kept the prices high to maintain its profits. And, of course, the British government was doing quite nicely through tea's taxation. Inevitably, when demand outstrips supply and when the price of the commodity is too high, an illicit trade will develop.

Tea smuggling boomed.

The Romantic Image of the Smugglers

It is a curious phenomenon, but when society feels that a government or big business is treating it unfairly or is holding a monopoly over certain commodities, a folk hero tends to arise. Take Robin Hood as an example. In old medieval England he was renowned for robbing the rich and giving to the poor. William Tell in fifteenth-century Switzerland did much the same. Both were excellent shots—Robin Hood with his longbow and William Tell with his crossbow. The railroads in America in the years after the Civil War saw Jesse and Frank James. Australia had Ned Kelley, the armor-clad outlaw. And behind all of them were bands of merry men or gangs of eager helpers. While these actual outlaws were not giving money to the poor; they were gaining popularity by robbing from the large organizations that people perceived to be making money off the public.

So too was it with tea smugglers. They were often feted as heroes, fighting against oppression, taking money from the rich— in this case, the British government or the East India Company—and giving it to the poor, or rather selling their smuggled goods at knock-down prices that common people could afford.

When a country is drained economically from a war, the government typically increases the taxes on its citizen to help finance the war. Thus, poor and working class citizens are usually required to do without certain luxury items. And it's during these times that smuggling increases. It was precisely this that happened in Britain in 1756, when the Seven Years' War began. At that time, the East India Company was importing not far from producing five million pounds (a little over two million kilograms) of tea per year. But the tea was too expensive for the majority to purchase, so tea smuggling was a profitable venture. For one thing, tea was a commodity that everyone seemed to want, the people despised the tax on it, and it was an ideal good to smuggle, being light and easily transported—far easier than heavy casks of brandy. In many cases, the people not only turned a blind eye to these smugglers, but rather they welcomed and aided them.

Big Business in Tea Smuggling

Ships smuggling tea to various destinations usually landed in secluded bays and coves and dropped their cargo to waiting smugglers who used the caves as warehouses and then conveyed their wares by horse caravans to distribution points around the local area. These smuggling gangs became larger, more organized, and more ruthless as success in their trade became greater. Their ships were typically armed, they were not afraid of the navy, and they were prepared to fight and even kill those who got in their way—mainly the customs officials, whose job required them to seize contraband.

The Hawkhurst Gang

The south coast of England became infamous for smuggling tea during the eighteenth century, and even today, many people hearken back to this time wearing rose-colored glasses. Smugglers are depicted by many as merry men who made their living by outwitting the doltish customs officers—often involved in skirmishes and fights in a fairy-tale pirate way. The reality, however, was a lot less glamorous, as evidenced by the horrors perpetrated by the Hawkhurst Gang.[19]

On September 22, 1747, customs officers intercepted a boat carrying two tons of illegal tea off the coast of Dorset in Southwest England. The customs men impounded the tea in a warehouse in the town of Poole. However, the smugglers, known as the Hawkhurst Gang, were not prepared to let their smuggled goods go so easily. The gang was not a bunch of merry men smuggling tea for altruistic reasons. They were instead hard-noised thieves who silenced local magistrates by burning down their property.

One day, sixty of the gang members raided the customs house and stole back the tea. Given their previous encounters (and victories) over the local magistrates, they did not take any precautions while riding North—not even bothering to disguise themselves or to conceal the stolen tea. The gang rode through a small village in Hampshire called Fordingbridge, with their spoils on the backs of packhorses. One of the smugglers, a man named John Diamond, even stopped and had a friendly conversation with Daniel Chater, one of the villagers. In parting, Diamond gave Chater a bag of tea.

But the bag of tea did not bring any sort of luck to Daniel Chater. Other villagers began to gossip about it, and news of the smugglers' procession reached the customs men, who were determined that such blatant disregard for the law could not go unpunished. The customs men descended on Fordingbridge, and Daniel Chater was pressured into testifying against John Diamond.

On February 14, 1748, a customs officer named William Galley rode with Daniel Chater toward Chichester to see a local magistrate. Along the way they stopped at the White Hart Inn in Rowlands Castle. Unknown to them, the landlady had two sons who were part of the Hawkhurst Gang. She sent word to them, and soon, gang members arrived at the bar, striking up conversation with Galley and Chater and getting them quite drunk. As the night progressed, the gang members discussed what they should do with the two men. It was finally decided that they should be punished, so they were beaten and horsewhipped and then tied to horses and taken fifteen miles to another village. The two men were exhausted and frequently slumped over and ended upside down under the horses bellies, suspended only by their legs, which were tied to the saddle. Both sustained kicks about their heads from the horses.

Galley begged to be killed quickly, for he had no doubt that the gang meant to execute them, but his pleas went unheard. The gang members continued to beat them; they were beaten so badly that by the time they arrived at the Red Lion Inn at Rake, Galley appeared to be dead. The smugglers buried him and then chained Chater in a turf house while they set about the serious task of heavy drinking and planning their alibis. They then left and returned to their homes, leaving Chater chained all the while.

Two days later, fourteen gang members returned to the Red Lion Inn to deal with Chater. They took him to a well with the intention of casting him down it. When the poor man fell to his knees and started to pray, one of the smugglers slashed Chater's face with a knife, almost cutting off his nose and blinding him. Chater tried to hasten his own end by jumping into the well, but he was stopped and instead hung inside the well. After fifteen minutes he was still alive, so the gang hauled him back out before tossing him headfirst down the shaft. But he survived even that, so they threw stones and logs at him until he stopped groaning.

In an attempt to conceal their tracks, the gang members killed Galley's horse, but Chater's had escaped. They then went back to their business, sure that no one would dare to give them away.

The authorities offered substantial rewards for the gang's capture, with the promise that the full force of the law would be used against the smugglers. Perhaps someone claimed a reward, for one member of the gang was arrested, and he agreed to give up the other gang members if he was granted leniency. The result was that the bodies of Galley and Chater were soon recovered. The full extent of the brutality of the smugglers was later revealed. Chater's body was viciously battered, and one leg had almost been severed. When they unburied Galley they found that he was in an upright position with his hands in front of his eyes. Seemingly, he had been buried alive, had attempted to dig his way out, but had ultimately succumbed to suffocation.

The public quickly lost its sympathy for the smugglers after news of the brutal murders was revealed. And the full force of the law was certainly used upon the gang. Eight of the ringleaders were tried and sentenced to death by hanging. One of them died before the sentence could be carried out, but he did not escape completely. His body was put in chains and hung as a warning for all to see.

From Smuggled Tea to the Boston Tea Party

In the previous chapter, we discussed some of the events leading up to the American War of Independence, including the Boston Tea Party. It must be added here that smuggled tea indirectly contributed to that historic event.

As mentioned at the beginning of this chapter, the East India Company was importing nearly five million pounds of tea to Britain each year in the mid-eighteenth century. Compare that with the 7.5 million pounds (3.5 million kilograms) of tea that was being smuggled into Britain; this meant that citizens were able to buy cheap tea on the black market, resulting in the East India Company accruing a huge surplus of unsold tea. This surplus increased greatly when the colonies refused to buy the tea from the company, but rather actively imported smuggled tea from Holland.

The East India Company was effectively on the point of bankruptcy, which the British government was not prepared to allow to happen. That is why the Tea Act of 1773 was so significant: It allowed the East India Company the right to sell tea directly to the colonists, bypassing the colonial wholesale merchants. This legally gave the company a means of reducing its surplus, since it could sell its tea cheaper than the colonial merchants, who had been dealing in the smuggled Dutch tea. The British government was quite content with this arrangement because it provided them with a means of collecting extra taxes from the colonists. Yet as we saw in the last chapter, this merely increased the dissatisfaction felt by the colonies about the British government's right to tax them.

William Pitt the Younger

William Pitt Jr. (1789–1806), also known in Britain as William Pitt the Younger, was a man of high stature in the eighteenth century. His father, the Earl of Chatham, had been Prime Minister twice before Pitt took over the position. He had wealth, intelligence, and powerful connections— and he was only twenty-four when he took office.

Pitt saw that the tax on tea was divisive, that it had led to the loss of the American colonies, and that it was lining the pockets of the smugglers rather than filling the government's coffers. Therefore, he introduced the Commutation Act of 1784, which reduced the tax on tea from 119 percent to a paltry 12.5 percent. This almost immediately halted tea smuggling and increased the consumption of imported East India tea. In fact, the reduction of the tea tax increased tea sales so much that the amount of tax that was collected increased dramatically and exceeded the amount that had previously been collected.

Is That Really Tea You Are Drinking?

During the illicit tea trade, many traders altered their product, making it less than 100 percent what they were advertising. People buying tea from smugglers many times were drinking tea that had been adulterated with all manner of dried herbs from the hedgerows of England. Hawthorn, elder, and ash leaves were commonly used as tea substitutes.

In 1725, the British parliament passed an act that banned the mixing of teas, but it proved unenforceable. Apart from smugglers, there were many people who made a living by altering tea and coffee and selling the leaves and beans to tea- and coffeehouses as well as to grocers and less discriminating restaurants.

Used tea leaves and coffee grounds were obtainable for a few pennies from hotels, coffeehouses, and teahouses and were made to look fresh by chemical treatments. In the case of tea, the leaves were often boiled with copperas (ferrous sulphate) and sheep's dung, and then colored with Prussian Blue (ferric ferrocyanide), verdigris (copper acetate), logwood, tannin, and charcoal. This produced what looked like good fresh tea—which may well have found its way back to the very hotels and teahouses that it had been bought from.

PART TWO

TAKING TEA

Chapter Seven

Types of Tea

If you are cold, tea will warm you;
If you are too heated, it will cool you;
If you are depressed, it will cheer you;
If you are excited, it will calm you.

—*William Ewart Gladstone (1809–1898),*
Prime Minister of Great Britain

WHENEVER YOU GO INTO A TEASHOP YOU MIGHT become overwhelmed by the bewildering varieties of tea available.[20] There are around fifteen hundred varieties worldwide, yet the startling fact is that all these varieties come from the same shrub: *Camellia sinensis.*

A Little Botany

If you thought that the different names of tea, derived from the different pronunciations of the character for tea—cha or tay—was complex, then gird your loins for a bit of botany.

Botanical taxonomy, or the way that plants are named, can be confusing. Latin is the language of science, and the system we now use was developed by Carl Linnaeus (1707–1778), a Swedish botanist, physician, and zoologist.

The white-flowered evergreen shrub that is the origin of all teas is a genus of *Camellia*, from the family *Theaceae*. The name *Camellia* comes from the Latinized name of the Reverend Georg Kamel (1661–1706), a Jesuit missionary to the Philippines who made substantial contributions to botany in the seventeenth century. Linnaeus gave the name in honor of Kamel, although he had nothing to do with the tea plant. *Sinensis* is Latin for "from China."

There are three main varieties of the shrub used for tea:

- *Camellia sinensis* var *sinensis*, which is used to cultivate Chinese, Japanese, and Formosan teas. It produces small leaves.
- *Camellia sinensis* var *assamica*, which is used to cultivate Indian and most other teas. It produces large leaves. (Although Darjeeling tea, which is grown in West Bengal, India, is grown from *Camellia sinensis* var *sinensis*.)
- *Camellia sinensis* var *cabodiensis*, which is a hybrid of the others and as such has a flavor intermediate between them. It is used to cultivate tea in Cambodia. It produces an intermediate leaf size between the other two major varieties.

If left to grow naturally, *Camellia sinensis* will grow into a tree up to 20 feet (6 meters) in height. And *Camellia sinensis assamica* can grow up to 40 feet (12 meters) tall. Clearly, those would make it difficult to harvest the leaves, so the plants are trimmed to keep them no larger than shoulder height.

Plant Morphology

- The alternately arranged leaves are longitudinally ovate. They have pointed tips and are finely serrated
- The blossom is white with five petals
- The scent is uniquely tea-like!
- The fruit is triangular and woody

Cultivation and Harvesting

There are several factors that determine the different types of tea.[21] These factors include:

- Altitude: Tea is usually grown between 985 feet (300 meters) to 6,500 feet (2,000 meters). The higher the altitude, the smaller the leaves and the smaller the plant. Obviously that will mean smaller harvests. The plant will even thrive at an altitude of 6,900 feet (2,100 meters), but some varieties can be grown at sea level.
- Climate: The tea plant needs tropical or subtropical rainforest conditions. They require at least fifty inches (127 centimeters) of rain per year.
- Soil mixture: Tea plants thrive in acidic soils.

Tea plants are propagated from both seeds and cuttings. It can take between four and twelve years until a plant is ready to produce seeds.

Generally, only one to two inches (2.5 to 5 centimeters) of the mature plant are picked. These buds and leaves are called the "flush." During the growing season, there will be a new flush every two weeks. This typically occurs in the spring and early summer.

The traditional way of harvesting the new shoots is to take only the top two leaves and one bud.

It's important to note that where the leaves are taken from, along with the presence or absence of the bud, can have a significant effect on the taste of the tea. Orange pekoe tea is made from the youngest open leaves, whereas Souchong tea is made from older leaves found closer to the woody stem.

Tea Processing

When we talk about the different types of tea, we are really referencing the categories that tea is put into according to the way the tea leaves are treated when they are processed in order to make brew-able tea.

The six different types of tea are as follows: white, green, yellow, black, oolong, and post-fermented, and they have the following properties:

- White, green, and yellow teas are unfermented;
- Oolong is semi-fermented;
- Black tea is fermented; and
- Post-fermented teas have gone through all of the processing and then are allowed a second fermentation under microbial activity. The best-known example is Pu-erh tea.

It is worthwhile to briefly discuss the processing method, as this will help explain exactly how the different types of tea are produced. Processing involves a variable amount of oxidation of the leaves, then the drying of the leaves. The amount of oxidation that is allowed during processing is the determining factor for producing unfermented or fermented teas.

Picking

There are two ways in which leaves are able to be picked: manually or by machine. Some plantations use a combination of the two. A skilled tea plucker can harvest 65 to 75 pounds (30 to 35 kilograms) of fresh tea per day. This would ultimately yield 15 to 20 pounds (7 to 9 kilograms) of dried, ready-to-use tea. A machine can do more, but it is not as skilled as a human. Thus, high-quality teas tend to be handpicked.

Withering or Wilting

Withering or wilting the leaves is the first step in the processing of tea. Tea leaves begin to wilt almost as soon as they are picked. This happens because enzymes within the leaves, once off the bush, begin a process called *enzymatic oxidation.* This means that natural catalysts called enzymes cause a degradation of the various chemicals and pigments in the leaves. This is one of the basic processes that cause fruits and vegetables to go brown when they are cut or opened.

Withering aids this process by encouraging the loss of moisture from the leaves and for oxidation to take place. This can be achieved either by spreading the leaves out and letting them dry in the sun or by using a withering room, where the leaves are laid out and a breeze is allowed to flow over them to facilitate evaporation of the moisture.

The leaves lose about a quarter of their weight during withering, and the oxidation breaks proteins down into amino acids, helping to release caffeine. This has an ultimate effect on the flavor of the tea.

Leaf Maceration

In maceration, the leaves are bruised to cause some further cellular damage and to enhance the oxidation. This is done by tossing or agitating the leaves on bamboo trays or by tumbling them in baskets.

Mechanization is often used to roll, beak, and macerate the leaves.

Oxidation and Fermentation

In the majority of tea literature, the words *oxidation* and *fermentation* are used interchangeably, but this is problematic, for they are two distinct things.

Oxidation in tea is a chemical process that takes place in the presence of oxygen, in which polyphenols are broken down by enzymatic reaction using the enzymes polyphenol oxidase and peroxidase and turned into theoflavins and theobromins. Fermentation is a microbial breakdown in the relative absence of oxygen.

The oxidation process results in the pigments in the leaves being broken down by enzymes. Tannins are then released. The more oxidation that takes place, the darker the leaves become.

This is the crux of the process since the fermentation process can be allowed to continue for a long period of time, or it can be switched off by heat as in the next process. These teas require the following oxidation periods:

- Oolong tea: allowed to oxidize between 5 to 40 percent

- Dark oolong: allowed to oxidize to 70 percent
- Black tea: allowed to fully oxidize and ferment

Fixation

Fixation is also known as "kill-green," and in this process, the leaves are heated in order to denature the enzymes, which stops the process. This can be done by heating the leaves in a wok or by steaming them. It can also be done industrially by baking the leaves in large drums.

Yellowing or Sweltering

This is a process only used on yellow teas. After the fixation process, damp leaves are heated in a closed chamber. This causes a yellowing of the leaves, as a result of alterations in the chlorophyll molecules and will produce the characteristic yellow tea.

Shaping

Shaping is a rolling or more complex process that produces shapes in the tea. Shaping can mold tea into strips, pellets, balls, spirals, or cones. Oolong tea leaves are often rolled into large balls the size of chestnuts and are sometimes mixed with other plants, like jasmine or lotus, to produce flavored teas.

Drying

Leaves are then dried to prepare it for its final journey to the consumer. Drying can be done by sunning, airing, or baking the tea leaves.

Curing

Curing is an extra step that is sometimes used to produce a second fermentation of the leaves. This is the case in the post-fermented Pu-erh tea.

All these parts of the tea-making process have been refined by different tea producers in order to produce just the right kind of tea with characteristic flavors. It is an incredibly skilled process that has been the subject of much scientific study, as befits this wonderful and amazingly versatile plant.

The Types of Tea

Now that we've learned how different tea leaves are picked and processed, it's worth mentioning each type of tea in detail.[22]

Yellow Tea

This unfermented tea is made exclusively in China and is a specialty of the Anhui, Sichuan, and Hunan provinces. Yellow tea is quite rare and is only just beginning to creep into the West among tea enthusiasts. It is also quite expensive and tends to be sold as bud and leaf tea.

The damp leaves are wrapped in paper and allowed to mellow and yellow for several days. They are then heat dried. The yellowness of the tea refers to the yellow-golden color of both the leaves and the brew.

The key taste words are mellow, sweet, and ripe. There may also be a slight lingering aftertaste. There are several varieties of yellow tea, including:

- Meng Ding Hu: one of the most famous yellow teas of China, made from tender leaf buds plucked from the peak of Mount Meng.
- Huan Shan: yellow sprouting, it is a spring tea.
- Huang Ya: also known as yellow broth.

White Tea

White tea is a specialty of the Fujian province in Southeast China. It is also grown in Darjeeling and Assam in India and in Sri Lanka. It is gradually finding a market in the West.

White tea is unfermented and only goes through two processes: withering and drying. The description "white" refers to the silvery-white downy feathers that are apparent on the leaves. The key taste words are sweet and mellow.

There are two main types of white tea:

- Yin Zhen: meaning "silver needles." This is often blended with jasmine.
- Pai Mu Tan: meaning "white peony." This is a bud and leaf tea.

Green Tea

This is the most well known of the unfermented teas. There are many types of green tea and it is becoming very popular in the West, especially as more and more research comes out in favor of its health-giving qualities.

Most of the green teas come from China and Japan, but they use different processing methods. In China, the plucked leaves are dried quickly to halt fermentation, and emphasis is placed on the rolling and shaping of the leaves. They are often rolled into long spirals or shapes that will gradually unfurl as they are steeped when the consumer makes the brew.

In Japan, the leaves are steamed in a large tank before being rolled and dried. This is often done several times before they are graded and sorted. The Japanese also make a very special green tea known as *matcha*. This is powdered tea, which is used in the Japanese tea ceremony.

The keyword for green tea is sweetness, though some are also slightly bitter.

There are many different types of green tea, including:

- Dragon Well: perhaps the most popular green tea in China. It is a spear-shaped leaf tea picked in pairs.
- Anji Bai Cha: has arrow-shaped and feathery leaves. It is fired early to stop fermentation, so it has a spring, young leaf flavor.
- Mao Jian: has sea-cultured leaves with silver tips. The tea has a nutty flavor.
- Pouchong: this has a rich, melon-like taste.
- Gunpowder tea: this is from China's Zhejiang province. The leaves are rolled into little balls shaped like gunpowder pellets. They unfurl as the tea is infused.

Oolong Tea

This is a semi-fermented tea. This word *oolong* actually means "black dragon" in Chinese. It comes from one of those delightful legends that have grown up around tea. As legend has it, a plantation owner once went to inspect his harvest but was driven away by the sight of an awesome black dragon. He stayed away for several days and was thankful to find that the black dragon had gone. The tea leaves, however, had gone quite dark, as they had been left to ferment in the sun. The tea was a revelation to him.

Of course, the name may have a less exciting origin, in that the leaves tend to unfurl into intricate flowing shapes, which can be used in tasseography, when the meaning of a black dragon in the teacup will be discovered (see chapter 18).

Oolong tea is sometimes also known as wu-yi tea because it has been harvested from Mount Wu-yi Shan in the Fujian province of China since the fifteenth century.

Oolong tea tends to be cultivated in China and Taiwan. Fermentation is permitted to about 30 percent in China and to about 60 to 70 percent in Taiwan.

The keywords for taste are fragrant, floral, and refreshing. The following are becoming more available in the West:

- Tie Guan Yin, Iron Buddha, or Iron Goddess of Mercy: this has a sweet, flowery scent and taste.
- Anxi Rou Gui, or cinnamon tea: has a delicious spicy flavor.
- Big Red Robe: this has a deep flavor that will cloak the mouth, hence the name.
- Dan Cong: sometimes known as the champagne of oolong tea. It can be very expensive. The flavors are similar to honey and apricot.
- Ali Shan: a Taiwanese tea. It is made into balls and produces a sweet flavor.
- Mao Xie King: this is known as Hairy Crab tea because its hairs resemble the Hairy Mud Crab, which is a delicacy in Anxi in Southern Fujian.

Black Tea

This is a fermented tea. It is the type of tea that people in the West are most familiar with. Black tea is grown in China, India, and Sri Lanka. It accounts for 90 percent of all the tea sold in the western world.

Black tea is known as red tea in China and Taiwan because of the reddish color of the brew. It is known as black tea in the West because of the color of the dried tea leaves.

Black tea is completely fermented, so it has gone through virtually all of the processes outlined earlier in this chapter.

Black tea can last longer than green tea or the other unfermented teas; hence, it was a more desirable trading tea in the early days of the tea trade, when cargoes moved about the world by ship. Even the "fast" tea clippers took weeks to get from trading port to trading port. Whereas green tea will only last a year, back teas can last several years.

India produces most of the world's black tea, which comes from the plant *Camellia sinensis* var *assamica*. There are many different varieties of black tea, which are cultivated to produce a vast range of tastes. Some are quite mellow and others are decidedly smoky.

The smoky teas are ones that have been dried over smoking wood fires. One story is that this was discovered by accident when some tea producers were late in processing their tea and tried to speed up the drying process by heating leaves over a fire. This was found to dramatically change the flavor of the tea, so it was added to the process.

Black teas are either pure or blended. Some people prefer the pure varieties, whereas others prefer the dependable taste that has been achieved by the blended types. Pure varieties are generally named after the region where they are produced.

Some Chinese and Taiwan pure varieties

- Lapsong Souchong: this is a tea from the Fujian province. It is dried over burning pine, which imparts a strong smoky flavor.

- Keemun: this is a tea from the Anhui province. It has a characteristic fruity aroma with a plum and flowery flavor.
- Dian Hong: this is a tea from the Yunnan province. It is a malty tea made from tea buds.
- Sun Moon Lake: this is a tea from Taiwan. It has a honey, cinnamon, and peppermint flavor.
- Tibeti: this is a tea from the Sichuan province. It is a famous Tibetan tea, which can be made into tea bricks.

Some Indian and Sri Lankan pure varieties

- Assam: this is a tea from Assam. It is full-bodied and malty.
- Darjeeling: this is a tea from West Bengal. It is floral and fruity, known as the champagne of black teas.
- Nilgiri: this is a tea from Tamil Nadu. It has a strong, aromatic flavor and a fragrant aroma.
- Ceylon: this is a tea from Sri Lanka. It is strong, rich, and full-bodied.

Blends are often common to certain areas and may also have other plants or flavors added to the tea. Examples of blended teas reflecting the region where they come from are:

- English Breakfast: this is blended from Assam, Ceylon, and Kenya teas.
- English Afternoon: this is blended from Assam, Ceylon, and Kenya teas.
- Irish Breakfast: this is blended from teas from Assam but often also with others.
- Earl Grey: this is a black tea flavored with oil of bergamot.
- Lady Grey: this is Earl Grey with lavender.
- Citrus Lady Grey: this is Earl Grey with Seville orange.

- Russian Earl Grey: this is Earl Grey with citrus peel, vodka, and lemon grass.
- Masala chai: this is black tea with spices, milk, and sweetener. It is a traditional drink in India.

Post-Fermented Teas

Post-fermented teas have been allowed to ferment in the open air for months or even years. This process allows further oxidation as a result of internal enzymatic action inside the leaves, but also additional microbial fermentation through contact with microbes in the air.

In China, these types of tea are called "black tea," because they are very black brews.

There are several types of post-fermented tea but they are not all made from black tea. Some are produced from green or oolong teas that are allowed to undergo this open-air fermentation process.

Pu-erh Tea

This post-fermented tea has been made since the time of the Tang dynasty. It is a dark tea that is made in China's Yunnan province. Pu-erh tea has a rich heritage and many legends surrounding it. Rather like green tea, it has been shown to have several health benefits, which we shall return to in chapter 14.

It is said that Pu-erh tea has been cultivated since the time of the Han dynasty (202 BC–220 AD), possibly even earlier. The name comes from Pu-erh County, itself named after Puerh City, where the tea was produced. The area most famous for this type of fermented tea is called Xishuan-banna, most specifically the "Six Famous Mountains." There, wild tea trees of great antiquity, some five hundred years old or more, were said to have once been harvested by monkeys trained by Buddhist monks. Another version of the tale is that monks threw stones at monkeys that perched in the branches of these trees and that in retaliation the monkeys tossed down tea branches. Interestingly, "Monkey Picked Tea" is a term that is still used today to denote high-quality tea.

The different mountains in the region all produce different types of Pu-erh tea.

The average temperature in this mountainous area is 60 to 70 degrees Fahrenheit (17 to 22 degrees Centigrade), with an annual rainfall of 45 to 70 inches (1,200 to 1,800 milimeters), quite ideal for growing tea.

Pu-erh tea means "living tea," and it is rich in microbes, rather like "live" yogurt. It is for this reason that for centuries Pu-erh tea has had a place in traditional Chinese medicine.

After picking, Pu-erh tea is put through a process of maturation involving withering, drying, and rolling to produce rough tea, which is called "moacha." It is a large broad leaf tea and two types of Pu-erh are produced:

- Green Pu-erh, or raw Pu-erh, tea, which is naturally fermented over many years; and
- Black Pu-erh, or cooked Pu-erh, tea, which is artificially fermented.

The Green Pu-erh tea is immediately pressed into cakes and left to mature for up to fifty years or more. The longer the tea is left, the more expensive it becomes, and tea connoisseurs may pay up to £1,000 ($1,500) per pound.

Black Pu-erh tea is speed fermented to age it over a period of up to sixty days. This involves turning the leaves every day, splashing them with water, covering them with cloth, and leaving them to ferment. After that, they are dried and pressed.

Flowering Teas

Flowering teas are worth mentioning, because many tea producers mix tea leaves while they are still moist with various types of flowers. They are then sewn with cotton thread into various shapes or bundles. This sewing process is skillfully done and very quickly, in about one to twelve minutes, depending upon the flower and the complexity of the bundle.

Jasmine blossom tea may take a mere minute to sew, while chrysan-
themum or osmanthus flower bundles may take up to twelve minutes.

These flower bundles then undergo the same processing as loose
leaves. When they are eventually ready for the consumer, one bundle is
simply placed in the pot and boiled water is added. The leaves open up
like a lotus or like whatever flower has been used in the process as the tea
brews. Watching the blossoming flower adds to the aesthetic experience
of such teas.

Grading Tea

After tea has been processed, it is then graded. Grading relates to the
quality of the leaves rather than to the quality of the drink brewed. There
are, however, different ways that tea can be graded throughout the world,
depending on the tea grower and the methods of processing accepted in
different tea-growing regions. Green tea and oolong teas, for example,
have a grading system that considers the variety of plant used, the region
it was grown in, and the stage of picking of the tea leaves.

The grading of black tea is fairly standard and involves two main
factors: leaf size and method of manufacture. In terms of leaf size, the
larger the leaves, the higher the grading. With regard to method of
manufacture, this is either done traditionally, by hand, or by mechanical
means, which involves crushing, tearing, and curling—often designated
as the CTC process.

The Five Main Tea Grades

There are five main grades of tea leaves, which include:

- Dust: the lowest grade. It is from the cut leaves and the smallest
  leaves.
- Fanning: mainly broken leaves. This is low-grade tea. It is the grade
  that is used for making tea bags, because it infuses very quickly.
- Broken Orange Pekoe: small leaves or large broken leaves. This is
  medium-grade tea.

- Orange Pekoe: large, whole leaves without flowers. This is high-grade tea.
- Flowery Orange Pekoe: whole tea leaves with flowery tips. This is high-grade tea.

The exact origin of the reason for using the word "orange" in grading these various teas is unclear. Some believe that it refers to the color of the brew, while others suggest that it has to do with the House of Orange, the Dutch royal house that gained the throne of Great Britain in the eighteenth century. The Dutch were, of course, heavily involved in the early trade in tea.

Pekoe comes from the Chinese word *pek-ho*, meaning "white hair," because fine white hairs, or down, are seen on the undersurface of some tea plants. This system is further refined by the addition of two qualities:

- Golden, where the leaves have a golden hue; and
- Tippy, when there is an abundance of buds present

Thus, abbreviations are used to immediately describe the tea. For example:

- GFOP stands for Golden Flowery Orange Pekoe. This is a tea with whole tea leaves, golden tips, and tea plant flowers.
- TGFOP stands for Tippy Golden Flowery Orange Pekoe. This is a tea including the buds and upper two leaves together with tea plant flowers.
- FTGFOP stands for Fine Tippy Golden Flowery Orange Pekoe.
- SFGFOP stands for Super Fine Golden Flowery Orange Pekoe. This is the highest grade possible.

Chapter Eight

Tea Tasting

I am so fond of tea that I could write a whole dissertation on its virtues. It comforts and enlivens without the risks attendant on spirituous liquors. Gentle herb! Let the florid grape yield to thee. Thy soft influence is a more safe inspirer of social joy.

James Boswell (1740–1795)

THERE IS MORE TO SIMPLY GRADING TEA AND PACKAGING it up in any old bag. The tea that starts its journey in some distant exotic tea garden still has a long way to go before it produces that delicious brew in your teacup. People have discriminating palates and know what they want from a cup of tea. Accordingly, tea manufacturers are prepared to go to inordinate lengths to package up their teas in order to give the consumer a reproducible drink that they will like and that will be consistent. In order to do this, they need people with super refined palates.

They need tea tasters.

A Sensitive Occupation

A tea taster has to know how to describe the flavor of a tea. Not only that, but a tea taster must use all of his or her senses to assess the quality of a tea. A tester looks at, touches, and crushes the leaves, listening to the sound that they make as this is done. A tester also smells and tastes the tea. Incredibly, a master tea taster can taste hundreds of teas in one hour.

That doesn't mean having a cup of each one but speed tasting and using a spittoon in order to move to the next.

A tea taster has to learn the craft, taking up to seven years to do so.[23] Once they have completed their training, they will be able to pinpoint where a tea has come from, the time of its harvest, and even which variety of plant it comes from.

Tea tasters are employed by tea blenders, tea sellers, and tea buyers. They are indispensible to the art of tea blending.

It Tastes of . . .

Tea tasters refer to the tea brew as the "liquor," and the vocabulary that tea tasters use is extensive and colorful. The following descriptors may be helpful for you when tasting your tea.

A taster will go down a line of teas, slurping each one as he tastes it. The slurping is the same as in wine tasting, whereby you draw air in over your lips, causing the tea to spray all over the palate. Please take great care, though, if you try this method, and never do so with hot tea. You could very easily burn yourself.

Most of the following descriptors refer to black teas:

- *Aftertaste*—the taste that is left in the mouth
- *Aniseed*—a flavor like the spice
- *Aroma*—the smell of the tea. You can also refer to a tea's "nose," or its "bouquet"
- *Astringent*—the tingle you get afterwards. This is similar to the feel of a clean mouth after a splash of mouthwash
- *Bakey*—the sense that it has been overbaked or overdried in processing
- *Berries*—a fruity flavor
- *Biscuity*—like bread or shortbread. A pleasant taste that is characteristic of Indian teas
- *Bitter*—an unpleasant taste may make you wince and want to reach for sugar

- *Body*—how substantial it feels. Generally, teas are light-, medium-, or full-bodied, rather like wines
- *Brassy*—a metallic taste
- *Bright*—its color, perhaps quite orange or coppery
- *Brisk*—it has a lively, refreshing taste
- *Chocolate*—a slightly sweet and chocolate-like taste
- *Clean*—it has a pleasant, fresh aroma and taste
- *Coarse*—it has a harsh flavor
- *Dull*—it is not clear to look at
- *Earthy*—it has an unpleasant, soil-like taste. This could be because the leaves became damp in storage
- *Flaky*—the leaves seem to have been damaged in processing
- *Flowery*—a high-quality tea
- *Golden*—the tips are present
- *Jam*—sweet, with an aftertaste like jam
- *Malty*—rather like whisky with a malt flavor
- *Plain*—quite featureless
- *Raw*—a bitter flavor
- *Stonefruit*—plum-like
- *Tobacco*—the smell of un-smoked tobacco
- *Vanilla*—quite a desirable flavor

And these descriptors are often used to assess green tea:

- *Bamboo*—like shoots of bamboo
- *Flowery*—can be differentiated into actual flowers, such as rose, jasmine, or lotus
- *Grassy*—like the smell of mown grass
- *Leek*—rather leek- or onion-like
- *Melon*—a fruity, refreshing flavor, similarly differentiated into types, such as sprite, watermelon, or honeydew
- *Nutty*—a pleasant nut flavor
- *Vanilla*—pleasantly fresh and desirable

Chapter Nine

Kettles, Caddies, Teapots, and Teacups

We had a kettle; we let it leak:
Our not repairing made it worse.
We haven't had any tea for a week . . .
The bottom is out of the Universe.
Rudyard Kipling, The Collected Poems of Rudyard Kipling

IN LU YU'S BOOK *CH'A CHING*, THE FIRST TEA MASTER describes twenty-eight utensils used to brew tea. It was a different method used then, of course, since the tea was boiled in a cauldron, rather than the steeping method that was developed during the Ming dynasty. Nowadays in the West many people simply use a kettle, a cup, a spoon, and a tea bag, which makes making tea more convenient and quick. Yet, there is much to be said for making tea in a more traditional manner, as we shall look at in chapter 10.

Kettles

Kettles, which are used all over the world purely for boiling water, have been around for millennia. An example of an early bronze kettle from Mesopotamia was found, dating back to around 3000 BC. It had a decorated spout, and archaeologists believe it was used as a cooking utensil.

The Chinese used cauldrons to boil water for drinking long before they started to brew and drink tea.

Exactly when kettles were used in Europe to exclusively boil water is not known, but it is likely that they were simply an adaptation of a cauldron that was heated over a fire. The addition of a spout made pouring a much simpler and more accurate business. At first, kettles were made of iron, but by the nineteenth century, copper kettles were in common use.

The electric kettle made its first appearance in 1891, when the Carpenter Electric Company of Chicago produced one that took twelve minutes to boil water. The heating element was in a separate boxed compartment at the base of the kettle. The Swan Company produced the first immersed element in 1922. This significantly sped up the boiling process. These electric kettles had to be watched, of course, since the kettle, if left unattended, could overheat and burn out. This was less of a problem once the Russell Hobbs kettle was developed in 1955, which incorporated an automatic switch-off mechanism.

James Watt's Kettle Idea

Scientific breakthroughs often come about in odd ways. Take the ancient Greek philosopher and mathematician Archimedes, for example. King Hieron of Syracuse had a crown made by a jeweler from a block of gold. Although the crown weighed the same as the block, Hieron was suspicious as to whether the jeweler had used all of the gold or whether he had substituted some silver. He handed the problem over to Archimedes, who was initially unable to come up with an answer, until one day, he got into his bath, and the solution presented itself to him. He realized that when a body is immersed in water, it would displace its own weight in water. Thus the Archimedes Principle was discovered, causing the great philosopher to run naked down the streets crying "Eureka!"[24]

Sir Isaac Newton, similarly, observed an apple fall to the ground and came up with the theory of gravity.

Around 1750, twelve-year-old James Watt had been watching his aunt's kettle boil and notice that as it bubbled away it caused the kettle to rattle and jump up and down. When he pushed the lid down firmly, the jumping stopped, but the steam came powerfully out of the spout. When he released the lid, the kettle bumped and rattled around again. He realized the immense potential power of steam, which he would put to great effect in improving the steam engine later in his life.

Tea Caddy

In order to keep tea leaves fresh, the tea caddy was created. All manner of receptacles are used to store tea and fit the name "caddy." They can include jars, boxes, tins, or ceramic containers.

The name "caddy" is thought to come from *catty*, which is a traditional Chinese unit of weight that is still used throughout East and Southeast Asia for weighing food. It is roughly 1 ⅓ pounds (over 1 kilogram).

Not surprisingly, the first caddies were imported from China and were made of porcelain. They were jars with porcelain lids or stoppers. Like the early imported teapots, they were often blue and white.

In the seventeenth and eighteenth centuries, as tea was a drink mainly for the wealthy, the tea caddies used in the West often reflected that wealth. They became a status symbol and could be made of the finest china or silver, and they were often engraved. Some families had three caddies—one for green tea, one for black, and one for a blend.

Most caddies included caddy spoons, again mainly made out of silver, and were often engraved with the family name. They were often quite ornate and are collectable nowadays.

Teapots

Teapots come in many weird and wonderful shapes and sizes, and in many different materials. They appeal to collectors around the world for pure aesthetics, and they appeal to tea enthusiasts and connoisseurs who seek out the best teapot for brewing and pouring tea. When you manage to obtain one that both looks good and pours well, you may feel that you have found the Holy Grail.

The oldest known teapot is housed in Flagstaff House in Hong Kong as part of the Museum of Tea Ware. It is said to have been made in 1513, and is attributed to Gonchung, said to be a master potter who worked for the Ming dynasty scholar Wu Yishan. It is dome shaped with a circular handle at the back and a tiny lid.

The most common type of teapot used to this day is the round one with a spout and curled handle. This was developed during the Ming dynasty. The Yixing clay teapot is the best example of such a teapot style that has been used continuously since the fourteenth century.[25] Yixing clay teapots are quite expensive to buy, but they make fantastic tea. They were traditionally made in and around the town of Yixing in the Jiangsu province on the east coast of China. The local clay is called *zisha,* and it is slightly purple in appearance. They are traditionally small and are used with accompanying small cups.

The beauty of the Yixing teapots is their slight porosity. They are generally used with black and oolong teas but can also be used for green and white tea. Typically, one would only use this type of teapot for one type of tea and stick with it rather than simply using it as a receptacle to try different teas in. And the teapot's porosity is the reason that it is generally used with only one tea. Gradually, the tea will seep into the clay and will build up a coating on the pot's interior. This helps to improve the flavor of the tea, and it is said that with very old ones, merely adding hot water will be enough to produce a cup of good, flavorsome tea.

Yixing teapots are small because they are based on providing a single serving of tea, as opposed to western teapots that may be used to serve four to six people. The traditional way of making these types of teapots is used to this day. That is, they are made by hand from a single sheet of clay. Many shapes are available, and if you are serious about searching out a great teapot, look for a Yixing.

A QUESTION OF CERAMICS

Ceramics are essentially inorganic, or nonmetalilic, materials used in daily life. They are the building blocks of society, quite literally, and include bricks, tiles, plates, glass, and even one of the most used seats in your home—your toilet!

It's important to include ceramics in our discussion about tea because many nonmetallic teapots are ceramic. This subject might vex tea historians and collectors as they try to date ceramic teapots, but it is worth discussing.

Virtually all nonmetallic teapots are ceramics and include:

- Pottery, which is made from coarse clay that is fired at low temperatures;
- Stoneware, which is made from better quality clay with fewer impurities and is fired at high temperatures; and
- Porcelain, which is made from pure kaolin clay and petunse rock fired at the highest temperature.

Teapot collectors tend to divide ceramics into just two types: pottery and porcelain. Porcelain can usually be differentiated from pottery as it is hard, translucent, and has a resonant ring when you ping it. Bone china is a type of porcelain made from kaolin clay and bone ash.

Porcelain Comes into Vogue

Porcelain was developed during the Sui dynasty (581–617), but it was used for drinking wine. It was not until the Ming dynasty that it was used to make teapots.

Once tea drinking caught on in the West, the demand for porcelain teapots soared. The East India Company imported the teapots around the globe, and thus, collectors call these pots "East India pots."

The East India pots were characteristically made in blue and white. At first the design used was a pear shaped, rather than apple-shaped, teapots with a straight spout. The reason for this was that the straight spout was considered easier for cleaning tea leaves. But later, someone had the bright idea to make a teapot with an built-in strainer at the base of the spout. From then on, the spouts tended to be made with a curve. And the more sophisticated they became, the more the curves became swan necked. And to this day, in dating teapots, collectors often look at the shape of the spout and the presence or absence of a strainer inside at the base of the spout.

English Silver

The oldest known English teapot is a tall silver ewer with a short straight spout, which looked rather like a coffee pot. It had a handle on the side so that it could be tilted easily simply by rotating the wrist. It was first commissioned by Lord George Berkeley and given to the East India Company in 1670. Lord Berkeley had it specially inscribed:

> This silver tea Pott was presented to the Comtee of the East India Company by the Right Honoe George Ld Berkeley of Berkeley Castle. A member of that Honourable and worthy Society and a true hearty Lover of them. 1670.

It is now on exhibition at the Victoria and Albert Museum in London.

Gradually, the designs of teapots changed, not just for aesthetic reasons but also for practical ones. A tall ewer-like vessel did not allow the brew to diffuse through to the top of the pot. The result was that the tea at the top was insipid, and at the bottom, it was far stronger. Consequently, silversmiths experimented with making small, rounder teapots. The first were ball or apple shaped. Then they adopted pear shapes with elegant swan-necked spouts. Then, towards the end of the eighteenth century, silversmiths started producing oblong-shaped teapots, which had large bases. Because of this extra large base, little trays or stands were made to rest the teapot on to protect the table.

In America, silver teaware was produced mainly in Boston. There were four main family firms: Revere, Edwards, Burt, and Hurd. The most famous of the Revere family was, of course, Paul Revere, whom we talked about in chapter 5. Not only was he a patriot and a leading figure in the Boston Tea Party, but he was also a creator of silver teapots. A fine example of this is to be seen in the portrait of him holding a teapot, painted by John Singleton Copley in 1768. It currently hangs in the Museum of Fine Arts in Boston.

Imari Teapots

Exports from China suffered after the fall of the Ming dynasty in 1644, when the kilns and porcelain factories at Jingdezhen in the Jiangxi province were damaged. The West's insatiable demand for porcelain needed to be satisfied, so the Dutch East India Company started to export Imari porcelain from Japan. These were highly colorful and beautifully decorated pieces that appealed to wealthy consumers in Europe. They were decorated with multicolored feathers, flowers, and exotic scenes.

Chinese Imari

Once the Qing dynasty was established, China tried to resume its export in porcelain, but the Imari style had captured the imagination of the West. Accordingly, Chinese porcelain producers started to copy the Japanese Imari style, and so Chinese teapots and teaware from this period is termed "Chinese Imari" to distinguish it from more traditional Imari.

Meissen

In 1708, Ehrenfried Walther von Tschirnhaus worked out a method of producing porcelain and started up the famous Meissen factory near Dresden, Germany. The company began to produce high-quality china, mainly styled after Chinese ware.

Teapots, and indeed all ware coming out of the Meissen factory, bear a hallmark of distinctive crossed swords. This stamp was started in 1720, in an attempt to stop imitators; it makes this one of the oldest trademarks in the world. Meissen dominated the European style of porcelain until the start of the Seven Years' War in 1756.

Wedgewood

In 1759, Josiah Wedgewood (1730–1795), the "father of English potters," established a pottery business in Burnslem, near the town of Stoke-on-Trent, in Staffordshire, England. Among other types of ceramic, he developed the famous "jasperware" and "black basalt." Jasperware was often used to make tea sets and is available in a number of colors, but most often in pale blue with designs of white atop it.

Tetsubin

The Japanese developed cast-iron pots with a spout and pouring handle.[26] In Japanese, this type of pot is written as 鉄瓶 meaning "iron kettle."

It is thought that this type of teapot was developed in the time of Sen no Rikyu, the great Zen tea master. Traditionally, the pots are heated over a charcoal fire on a brazier called a binkake, which means "hanging bottle."

Samovar

> В Ту́лу со свои́м самова́ром не е́здят
> Don't take a Samovar to Tula.
>
> Anton Chekhov (1860–1904)

The samovar epitomizes Russian tea drinking. It is an urn-shaped metal container used to heat water to prepare tea. It means "self-boiler."

The container has a spigot or tap near the base, handles at the sides, and a metal pipe that goes up through the body. The pipe is filled with solid fuel, such as pinecones, charcoal, and wood chips, which are ignited. A small teapot is used to brew a tea concentrate. This is often placed on top of the samovar to keep it heated with the passing hot air. Samovars are traditionally made out of copper, brass, nickel, or silver.

The tea concentrate is poured into each cup, and water is released through the spigot or tap. Families would traditionally sit around the table drinking tea with the samovar in the center.

It is said that the samovar has a soul, on account of the way that it sings as it heats the water. Many curious sounds emanate from it. The oldest samovar known was made of pottery and found in Azerbaijan dating to 1700 BC. The first copper one was made by the Lisitsyn brothers in 1778, in Tula, a city famous for its metalwork. By the mid-nineteenth century, Tulan samovar makers were producing 120,000 pots per year. This was a complex process involving twelve separate stages, each performed by a specialist. Apparently, whole villages could be involved in a single stage, such as making the pipe or the handles. These were then assembled in factories.

Nowadays, electric samovars are manufactured in Russia, but the traditional samovar often still holds pride of place.

Tea Sets

The first complete silver tea set was produced in 1790, but it was not until Queen Victoria's time (1819–1901) that a tea set was organized into a standard design of six cups and saucers, six teaspoons, a sugar bowl and sugar tongs, a milk jug, and a teapot. From then on, tea sets became standard in most homes in Britain and were the expected wedding present for British couples.

Teaspoons

The teaspoon was a necessary invention. When tea was introduced into the West, these spoons were very small, as were teacups and teapots, because tea was expensive. As the price dropped over the years, the size of teapots, teacups, and teaspoons all increased. By the 1730s, the size of the teaspoon became more or less standard and became a useful measuring device. A level teaspoon is accepted as one third of a level tablespoon. A heaped or a rounded teaspoon is quite imprecise, yet it is often used in cooking and tea making.

We shall return again to the subject of teaspoons in chapter 15, since these are quite useful and interesting objects in the tea lab!

Apothecaries' Measurement—A Source of Confusion

In days gone by, an apothecary was a mixer and a practitioner of medicine. While not being held as high up the social ladder as the university-educated physician, he was nonetheless the main doctor for the lower and middle classes.

Weighing out ingredients for remedies was a complex business, and a whole system of Apothecaries' measures were used:

> One pound = 12 ounces
> One ounce = 8 drachms
> One drachm = 3 scruples or 60 grain

An apothecary's teaspoon was used to measure one fluid drachm. This was equivalent to a quarter of a tablespoon.

When the household teaspoon size increased, it became the equivalent of a third of a tablespoon, as it remains to this day. The apothecary's teaspoon, however, remained the same measure.

One could imagine the potential dangers that might ensue with drugs, many of which were extremely toxic, if the wrong spoon was used.

Tea Infusers

The ingenuity of tea drinkers knows no bounds, and a whole range of tea infusers have been developed over the years. Infusers were very popular in the early nineteenth century and were used to infuse loose tea in a cup rather than in a pot. They were labor-saving devices and were regarded as convenience items for when one was on the move and had no way to use or transport a bulky teapot.

Tea infusers come in various shapes and sizes. The most popular are called tea balls or tea eggs. They consist of a tong-like arrangement with a metal ball or egg that is suitably perforated or has a mesh. Some consist of the ball on a small chain, which can be dangled over the side of the cup into the hot water.

The History of the Tea Bag

We cannot leave our discussion of tea receptacles without looking at the most significant and important development in tea drinking to have been made during the last century. I refer, of course, to the invention of the tea bag.

In 1908, Thomas Sullivan, a New York tea merchant, started to send out samples of his tea in small silken bags. Many of his customers assumed that the bag had to be soaked in the teapot instead of being emptied into the teapot, rather like the aforementioned tea infusers. It was due to this that the tea bag was born.

Entrepreneur that he was, Sullivan quickly realized the potential of this new product and began to produce bags with larger perforations than the silk mesh. He used gauze and produced the first custom-made tea bags.

In the 1920s, tea bags really took off in the market. Two sizes were made—large ones for a teapot and smaller ones designed to be used in a teacup. The bags had a string attached with a paper label, which could be hung over the side of the cup until the tea had infused, when it could be easily removed.

The British did not really grasp the invention and stuck to loose tea until after World War II, when austerity measures kicked in. Convenience products and labor-saving devices became deeply entrenched in the British psyche and the time became ripe for the tea bag. In 1953, Tetley introduced the tea bag to Britain, and other tea producers soon followed suit. It was slow growth, however, and after a decade, tea bags had only gained 3 percent of the tea market in Britain. This figure has increased year by year, so that now in the twenty-first century, tea bag make up 96 percent of the market in the UK. Compare that with 65 percent in the United States.[27]

Chapter Ten

Tea Rituals and Ceremonies

Teaism is a cult founded on the adoration of the beautiful among the sordid facts of everyday existence. It inculcates purity and harmony, the mystery of mutual charity, the romanticism of the social order. It is essentially a worship of the Imperfect, as it is a tender attempt to accomplish something possible in this impossible thing we know as life.

Kakuzō Okakura (1862–1913), The Book of Tea

There are few hours in life more agreeable than the hour dedicated to the ceremony known as afternoon tea.

Henry James (1843–1916), The Portrait of a Lady

THE WAY IN WHICH PEOPLE TAKE TEA VARIES AROUND the world. The Japanese tea ceremony is the most intricate and probably takes the longest, whereas the British often wake up to their tea maker, as it switches on the radio to wake them up and instantly pours their first cup of the day. It's time to journey around the world and examine the tea customs around the globe.[28]

China

It is appropriate to begin our journey by looking at tea drinking in the land that gave tea to the world. I mentioned at the beginning of this book that I first developed an interest in tea after I read the detective novels by the Dutch diplomat Robert van Gulik featuring Judge Dee—the Sherlock Holmes of ancient China. The novels are set during the Tang dynasty, which is significant in the history of tea, as we discussed in chapter 2.

Tea is very important to the character of Judge Dee. He uses it to ponder over cases, to interview suspects, or simply to relax. The method of brewing the tea is assuredly that of the Ming dynasty. There is an interesting exchange between the judge and Master Crane Robe, a Taoist recluse, during a tea ceremony in the novel *The Chinese Maze Murders*. By doing so, the author shows how tea drinking is associated with contemplation and intellectual pursuits.

Teahouses

Public teahouses became a feature of Chinese life as early as the Tang dynasty. Of course, like so many traditions, the visiting of teahouses was suppressed during the Cultural Revolution because these places were considered subversive. Thankfully, teahouses started to flourish again, and they are once more an integral part of Chinese society.

Yum Cha 饮茶

Yum cha is an informal type of tea drinking. It literally means "tea-tasting," and it usually takes place in the morning or the afternoon. Tea is served from a pot into tiny porcelain cups and is taken along with *dim sum,* meaning "heart treats." Usually dim sum are small savory snacks. Yum cha includes a sort of informal chat at a teahouse that friends or businessmen alike may indulge in.

Chaou Tea

Chaou tea is used for both informal tea drinking and for tea tasting, as well as for a slightly more formal type of tea drinking. It involves using a *gawain*, a lidded bowl or a covered bowl. It was first used during the Ming dynasty. It consists of a bowl, a lid, and a saucer, all usually made of porcelain. It can also be made from glass, from Yixing clay, or even from jade.

Tea leaves are steeped in the uncovered gaiwain bowl. It is ideally suited to more delicate types of tea, like green and white tea. In the cases of green or whie tea, the gaiwain tends to be used without the lid, but with oolong tea (semi-fermented tea) the lid is used. It is less often used for black teas, since the large surface area of the bowl cools the tea too much.

The lid is used to concentrate the flavor and also to use as a strainer to prevent the leaves from going into a cup, if it is being decanted. Sometimes tea is drunk directly from the gaiwan.

To drink from the gaiwan, both hands are used, and all three parts are used at once so that the right hand supports the saucer and holds the bowl while the left holds the bowl and the lid, either to decant into a cup or to drink direct.

Kung Fu Tea Ceremony 工/功夫茶道

This is the formal Chinese tea drinking ceremony. It is called Gongfu Cha Dao, IGongfucha, or the Kung Fu tea ceremony. The ceremony is done according to a set format with small Yixing teapots. These are tiny and only have a volume of about five fluid ounces. This creates a rounded flavor for the tea.

It is the sort of tea ceremony that one would use to welcome guests, or to pay respects to parents. Taoism has influenced the development of the ceremony, which represents harmony of nature epitomized by the preparation, drinking, and sharing of tea. It is ideally suited to oolong tea but can also be used with Pu'erh tea.

Japan

The famous Japanese tea ceremony—the Way of Tea, or *chanoyu*—is the traditional way of preparing matcha, the Japanese powdered green tea.

Matcha can be enjoyed in many different ways, as a drink and as a flavoring in beverages or food. The preparation of matcha is fairly labor intensive, but when it is done correctly, it is an experience that is worth the trouble. Matcha is drunk hot and involves whisking the tea into a smooth, creamy green drink.

There were several prominent tea masters who contributed to the development of the Japanese tea ceremony. The Zen tea master Sen no Rikyu (1522–1591) developed four guiding principles for the ceremony:

- Wa: harmony 和
- Kei: respect 敬
- Sei: purity 清
- Jaku: tranquility 寂

The teahouse—the place to perform the tea ceremony—demanded a stylized architecture called *chaseki*. This was essentially a small cottage with a low ceiling, a bamboo floor, and a hearth. Scrolls were often hung on the walls.

In traditional homes, a special tearoom, a *cha-shitsu*, is present, and people must enter the room on their knees to show humility.

Matcha can be served thick or thin. Tea ceremony guests share the thick tea, while the thin tea is usually poured into individual cups to enjoy.

The tea apparatuses for Japanese tea ceremony include:

- Chakin—a white linen cloth used to wipe the tea bowl
- Chawan—the tea bowl. These may be antique bowls made by famous tea masters
- Natsume—the tea caddy containing the matcha tea
- Chashaku—the tea scoop. This is a single piece of bamboo, wood, or ivory with a curved end to take out a quantity of tea
- Chasen—the tea whisk. This is made from bamboo and resembles a shaving brush, but is made from a single piece of bamboo

The tea ceremony is a very involved process. The guests are invited to the ceremony and are given some roasted barley tea upon their arrival. They are then welcomed by the host, bowing to each other. The guests are invited to wash their hands and rinse their mouths. Next, they remove their shoes and enter the tearoom via a small door. The actual ceremony can last several hours and the ritual is followed, governed by custom and politeness.

The kimono, a traditional Japanese garment, may be worn at the ceremony.

GEISHA 芸者

Geisha means "performing artist." Geishas are traditional Japanese entertainers who act as hostesses, often during the tea ceremony, and who dance, sing, and play classical Japanese music.

The Essence of Making Matcha

You can enjoy matcha without attending a Japanese tea ceremony. You can improvise with all of the equipment that you need, including the whisk. Just use a very small metal whisk and follow these instructions:

- Add ⅔ teaspoon (2 grams) of matcha tea into a small bowl.
- Pour a small amount of cold water over the matcha tea, and then use your whisk to tap out any lumps and make a paste. Note that cold water is needed here, not hot, or you will not get rid of the lumps.
- Add ¼ cup (60 milliliters) of hot water that has not boiled. It needs to be about 175 degrees Fahrenheit (80 degrees Centigrade).
- Hold the bowl with one hand and begin to whisk the tea. You should use a wrist action in an M-shape pattern with the whisk, keeping it running through the tea rather than scraping and bumping the bottom of the bowl. Do this quite vigorously for thirty seconds to one minute.

- When all of the large bubbles have been replaced by a thick foamy liquid, the matcha is ready.
- Drink, contemplate, and enjoy!

Korea

Zen Buddhism influenced the development of the tea ceremony in Korea. Monks would offer tea in a little ritual to the Buddha three times a day, and teahouses were often built in or near monasteries. In time a more secular type of tea drinking arose, and teahouses were established near springs so that they could be sure of using the best water.

The traditional Korean tea ceremony is called *darye*. It means "etiquette of tea" and is less formal than the Japanese tea ceremony. In addition, there are fifteen known Korean tea ceremonies, with a gradation of importance, from the daily drinking of tea in an informal setting to the greeting of ever-more important guests to inviting the queen and crown prince.

Korean teas are divided into five types according to taste: bitter, sweet, astringent, salty, and sour.

In a Korean teahouse, the tea is taken at a low table, around which the tea drinkers sit cross-legged. The tea master or the hostess pours warm tea into previously warmed cups. This is done from a distance of a few inches in order to produce a froth, which is regarded as a sign of good fortune and will give the drinker luck.

Taiwan

Tea drinking and ceremonies that have developed over the centuries in Taiwan are obviously heavily influenced by Chinese culture. There are three principal ceremonies for tea in Taiwan.

Wu-Wo Tea Ceremony

Wu-Wo means "no individual independent existence." That may sound pretty heady to the Western reader, but it reflects the purpose of the ceremony, which is to encourage the tea drinker to forget about knowledge, wealth, and appearance. The purpose of this ceremony is meditative—to transcend these things that tie us down to the banal and the unimportant.

The Lu-Yu Tea Culture Institute, named after Lu-Yu, the tea sage, was founded in Taipei, Taiwan, in 1980, and offers certificates for tea masters. It has schools in Beijing, Chengdu, and Shanghai.

Perennial Tea Ceremony

This tea ceremony is steeped in traditional philosophy, with the members of the ceremony taking the roles of the elements along with the host or tea master. It celebrates the seasons, the five elements, and yin and yang.

Gongfu Tea Ceremony

This type of ceremony is exactly the same as the Chinese tea ceremony. Most households in Taiwan will have a tea set consisting of a small earthenware teapot with small cups. Generally oolong tea has a short brewing time to allow the sweet flavor of the oolong to be appreciated without too much bitterness, which comes from a longer infusion. Ideally, spring water is used at just below boiling point. The kettle is taken off the heat when bubbles start to rise.

The cups are placed in a circle on a water tray. The tea is poured out in a continuous circular manner over the cups so that each cup will receive an identical drink rather than the last person receiving the strongest brew.

After pouring, the teapot is filled again with more water, it is common to have five or six such brews during the ceremony.

Bubble Tea

Bubble tea is gradually spreading around the world, with bubble teahouses mushrooming from Hong Kong, the Philippines, the United Kingdom, and all the way across America to California.

Bubble tea was invented in the 1980s, in Taiwan. Children returning from school often stopped off for a cup of tea. One tea concession holder started adding fruits to the milky tea to give it more flavor. The woman shook the tea and fruit up to mix it all up and it produced a bubbly brew. This proved so popular that other tea sellers started doing the same, gradually adding different items to sweeten the drink. Someone added tapioca pearls, which sank to the bottom, like sunken frog's spawn. Thus the tea looked as though it had bubbles at the bottom and bubbles at the top. Hence, bubble tea was invented.

Bubble tea is known by many names, including pearl tea drink, boba drink, boba ice tea, zhen zhou nai cha, tapioca ball drink, and many others. Bubble tea is taken cold or piping hot, and there are two main types: fruit-based and milk-based. The original bubble tea is made with hot Taiwanese black tea, tapioca pearls, condensed milk, syrup, or honey. The ingredients are all mixed together in a clear container with a domed top and a huge straw so the tapioca pearls can be consumed.

Pakistan, India, and Sri Lanka

Tea as a drink is popular throughout South Asia and is consumed at breakfast, lunch, and dinner. In Pakistan, both green and black tea are consumed, whereas India and Sri Lanka tend to drink black tea only.

The British rule of the continent during colonial days saw many British customs being absorbed into Indian culture. British women who visited the country, often in pursuit of a husband, introduced the British habit of taking high tea to the locals. High tea is a meal of sandwiches and cakes taken with tea served with milk and sugar. In time, it was superseded by *tiffin*, an afternoon small meal when rice, dosas, idlis, and sweet chapattis were eaten.

High tea is often served black with lemon, and sometimes just black with milk. In addition, there is also masala chai tea. Street tea vendors, called *chai wallahs*, push handcarts with a huge tea urn on top from whence they pour their tea into glass cups for a few rupees a shot. Masala chai is made by boiling the tea leaves in water with milk, sugar, and spices. The resulting beverage is strained before serving.

There is no fixed recipe, and many families come up with their own way of preparing it. The spices used include ginger, cinnamon, cloves, cardamom, and pepper.

Chai has spread around the tea-drinking countries of the world and is quite popular in the West. In the United States, it is often taken cold or iced and is sometimes topped with whipped cream.

In Sri Lanka, black tea is consumed with heated milk. If you stay at a hotel in Sri Lanka, you will often be given a wide choice of their teas at tiffin time.

Egypt

The people of the land of the pyramids hold tea in high esteem and consider it their national drink. Egyptians drink roughly 2.5 pounds (1 kilogram) of tea per person per year. They call it chai or shai.

In Upper Egypt, the ritual of shai is common among men who meet around a desert fire. They drink the shai and smoke flavored tobacco in a hookah waterpipe. The Egyptians tend to like black teas from India and Sri Lanka. The two types they typically make are koshary, which is most popular in Lower Egypt around the delta areas; and saiidi, which they drink in Upper Egypt. Koshary is black tea sweetened with cane sugar and mint. Saiidi is black tea that is boiled to concentrate it and then sweetened with cane sugar. It almost has a syrupy consistency.

Morocco

If you are ever in Morocco or dine at a Moroccan restaurant, be sure to finish your meal off with a maghrebi mint tea. The Moroccans typically use gunpowder green tea with mint leaves (or pine nuts if mint is not available). Sugar is added to the pot and boiled, which gives the tea a distinct taste. The mint is then generally removed, since it is a carminative and can cause heartburn.

The tea is poured from a distance, generally arm's length, in an impressive waterfall into the cup. It is traditional to take three servings of it.

The longer one takes to drink the brew, the stronger each glass is and the fuller the flavor.

There is an Algerian proverb that explains Moroccan tea:

> *The fist glass is as gentle as life,*
> *The second glass is as strong as love,*
> *The third glass is as bitter as death*

Russia

Alexander Sergeyevich Pushkin once said, "Ecstasy is a glassful of tea and a piece of sugar in the mouth." And as we learned in chapter 9, the Russians use the samovar to prepare tea. The tea concentrate is poured into the cup and then topped off with water from the samovar. The Russians do not use milk and do not add sugar to their tea. One way of sweetening the drink is simply to hold a sugar cube between one's teeth and drink through it, as talked about by the great Alexander Pushkin. It is quite a unique way of drinking tea and is very enjoyable.

The great Russian poet of the Romantic era, Alexander Pushkin, gives us this delightful little vignette of the samovar in his verse novel *Eugene Onegin*:

> Day faded; on the table, glowing,
> the samovar of evening boiled,
> and warmed the Chinese teapot; flowing
> beneath it, vapor wreathed and coiled.
> Already Olga's hand was gripping
> the urn of perfumed tea, and tipping
> into the cups its darkling stream—
> meanwhile a hallboy handed cream.

Europe

Coffee still dominates a lot of the countries on the European continent, but tea definitely has its enthusiasts among the Europeans.

France

Here you will find *salons de thé*, tearooms, which usually serve only black teas. The French tend to take their tea sweet or with lemon in the afternoons, accompanied by pastries.

Germany

The Germans have a unique tradition of taking their tea. A type of rock sugar called *kluntjes* is added to a cup, which is slow to melt and is left to sweeten several cups. This is then covered with black tea. Finally, a heavy cream is poured on top so that you have three tiers of tea, representing the sky, the water, and the land. It is unstirred and drunk so that you taste the cream first, then the tea, and then sweet tea as the sugar gradually infuses through. It is said to be medicinal and good for stress, headaches, and abdominal pains.

Ireland and the United Kingdom

The old-fashioned plan of allowing a teaspoonful to each person, and one over, is still practised. . . . When the infusion has been once completed, the addition of fresh tea adds very little to the strength; so if more is required, have the pot emptied of the old leaves, scalded, and fresh tea made in the usual manner.

Isabella Beeton (1836–1865), *Mrs. Beetons Book of Household Management*

Per capita, the Irish are the second highest consumers of tea in the world after the United Kingdom. Both countries are renowned as tea addicts. Builder's tea is how much of the population of Britain now take their tea. Builder's tea is strong black tea with milk and sugar. The common joke is that it needs to be so sweet that you can stand your spoon up in it.

That is not to say that everyone drinks tea like that in Ireland and the United Kingdom. There is a real demand for the many types of tea, and there are lots of specialty tea suppliers who will sell all types of loose-leaf tea to the purist tea drinker who wants to make tea in the proper, traditional manner.

So what exactly is that proper manner? While there is no exact way of preparing ea, the following is the traditional British way of making black tea, using either loose-leaf tea or tea bags (1 teaspoon of loose-leaf tea is the same as a small tea bags).

Tea apparatus to make a pot of black tea for two

- teakettle
- teapot
- 3 tsp of black tea

Method

1. Clean out the teapot and kettle.
2. Fill the kettle with water and boil it.
3. Pour a small amount of boiled water into the teapot to heat it. Swirl it around and then discard.
4. Place 1 teaspoon of tea per person into the pot and an extra "one for the pot."
5. Add about 1 ¼ cups (300 milliliters) of water person. Allow this to stand for three to four minutes.
6. Ask how your guest likes his or her tea, with milk first or last or with lemon.
7. Assuming the person wants milk, add a little, about ¼ to ½ inch (½ to 1 ¼ centimeters), in the bottom of the cup.
8. Strain the tea through a tea strainer.
9. Ask your guest if he or she would like sugar, and if so, hand him or her the bowl with sugar tongs if sugar lumps or with a teaspoon if granulated sugar.
10. Enjoy!

To make a pot of green tea, remember that you do not boil the water. It is best at about 175 degrees Fahrenheit (80 degrees Centigrade). No milk or sugar is added.

The United States of America

The Boston Tea Party might have made Americans loathe tea forever, but judging by the quantity of tea that is consumed to this day, that is far from the case. As we learned earlier, George Washington was a regular tea drinker, and Paul Revere was a maker of the most elegant silver teaware. Thomas Sullivan, the New York tea merchant, invented the tea bag, which revolutionized and sped up the tea-drinking habit. With the rise of the tea bag, tea could be made quickly without all the bother of heating teapots, using strainers, and having to dispose of used tea leaves.

Up until World War II, Americans drank green, black, and oolong tea. Green and black teas were drunk in equal measures, with oolong taking up about 20 percent of the total consumption. Inevitably, the war cut off green tea importation from China and Japan, with the result that black tea from India and Sri Lanka, two countries under British control, became the favored drink. Now black tea consumption accounts for 99 percent of the American tea-drinking market.

Generally, about 80 percent of American tea drinkers prefer to have iced tea.[29] Indeed, it is the great drink of the South. It is usually served as a sweetened drink, with sugar or other sweeteners added. The invention of iced tea is usually credited to a merchant named Richard Blechynden at the 1904 St. Louis World's Fair. He owned a tea plantation and was aiming to give away samples of his hot tea. However, the temperature outside during the fair was very high, and he had few takers. He therefore cooled his tea down by chucking ice into each glass, which cooled it. The iced tea was a great hit and has been a staple American drink since.

Some believe, however, that Blechynden did not actually invent iced tea, as there is an article that appeared in the *Nevada Noticer* in 1890, which referred to the Missouri State Reunion of Ex-Confederate Veterans held on September 20 and 21, 1890, at Camp Jackson. They held a huge barbeque, which was washed down by 2,220 gallons of coffee and 880 gallons of iced tea.

In addition to black, green, oolong, and iced tea, two imported variants have made great inroads into the American market as of late. India's masala chai is sold as chai tea across the country. And Taiwan's bubble tea has also found its home in the American tea-drinking market. In America, all roads lead to tea.

Some Tea Customs and Superstitions

There are many interesting customs and superstitions associated with tea drinking around the world. Many of these I learned about around my family's tea table while I was growing up.

Chinese Engagement

In China's traditional arranged marriages—made to continue ancestral lines and to create family alliances—after a betrothal was agreed, there would be an exchange of presents between the two families. The boy's parents would send money, tea, and dragon and phoenix bridal cakes. The tea was considered of such importance that all the gifts were referred to as *cha-li*. If the tea was accepted by the girl's family, the two were considered officially engaged.

Chinese Weddings

In China, it is traditional for the bride and groom to share a single cup of tea at the wedding. It is also keeping with tradition for them to kneel before their parents and prepare tea for them in gratitude for all that they have done for the newlyweds.

Respect Tea

In China, it was typical for younger generations to make tea for the older generations, as it was a tradition to make tea for one's boss. Things are no longer so prescribed in China, yet many still observe the custom, especially during Chinese New Year. This is a way for the younger generation to thank the older generation for their wisdom and guidance.

Saying Sorry

Tea can also function as a sign of apology. The apologetic party will often make tea after an argument.

The Correct Way to Express Appreciation Over Tea

When tea is poured for you in China, it is customary to show your thanks by gently tapping the table with your index and middle finger. This is a tradition extending back for centuries and is said to date to the early days of the Ching dynasty (1559–1911), when the emperor liked to dress casually and visit his people. His servants were instructed to give nothing away, and so they had to treat him as an equal. One day, in a teahouse, the emperor poured himself a cup of tea and also poured one for his servant. The servant immediately went to kneel before him, a gesture that is called *kou tou* (in English this has become the word "kowtow"). The emperor prevented him, for that would give their secret visit away. So instead, the servant made a kowtow with his two fingers. To this day, this is still used in China as a mark of appreciation when served tea or having your tea refilled.

English Women and Tea

The English have an old superstition that states: "Two women must not pour from the same teapot." According to the superstition, if two women do pour from the same pot, an argument is sure to ensue shortly thereafter.

Tea Leaves and Salt

Dating back to sixteenth-century England, in some parts of the country it was customary to scatter dry tea leaves and salt on the front doorstep to prevent evil spirits from entering a house.

Spilt Tea

The old superstition about bad luck following if salt is spilled—unless some is thrown over the left shoulder—is well known. This superstition arose from several myths, one being the depiction of Judas Iscariot spilling salt in Leonardo da Vinci's *The Last Supper*.

Spilt tea, however, was regarded in nineteenth-century England as a propitious sign and that if tea leaves were spilled, a blessing would fall upon the household.

Weak Tea and Strong Tea

In Scotland, if brewed tea turned out to be too weak, this was once taken as an omen that a friendship would be weakened.

Not surprisingly, if tea was made stronger than intended, this could indicate that a new friendship was in the making.

Only Use a Spoon to Stir the Pot

In Scotland, it is considered bad form to stir a pot of tea or even a cup of tea with anything other than a spoon. The handle of a fork or knife is rumored to stir up trouble for the stirrer!

Two Spoons

In Scotland, when setting a table or arranging things for tea, if two spoons are inadvertently placed on the same saucer, it is taken as an indication that the drinker will marry twice, or if a young girl, that she would one day have twins.

A Strange Leaf

In Scotland, if a single leaf floated to the surface of the tea, it was taken as a sign that a stranger would come into one's life.

A Stranger at Your Door

In Ireland and Scotland, if the lid of a teapot was left off and tea poured from the pot, it was said to indicate that a stranger would soon come to your door.

Tea Spouting

In England, if tea spills from the spout as the teapot is being carried, it is said to be a sign that a secret was about to be spilt.

Romance Bubbling

In Scotland and England, if bubbles formed on the surface of the tea, it indicated that romance was bubbling away. In this context, each bubble represented a kiss. An alternative explanation was that it represented money; the more bubbles the more money.

On the Sea

When British fishermen or sailors handed tea to their fellow comrades, it was considered bad luck to do so through a porthole or through the rungs of a ladder. It was also considered bad luck to empty the tea leaves from the pot while on a fishing boat. The more leaves that accumulated in the pot, the better the catch. Also, if the pot was washed out, it could be an omen that the ship would sink.

Fishing families in Scotland did not empty the teapot leaves or wash out the teapots while fishermen were at sea, in case they might be washed overboard and drown.

I'll Be Mother

This expression is often heard in the United Kingdom, meaning who will pour the tea. It stems from old fertility desires. A woman who wanted to have a child would pour the tea in order to help conception and to finally become a mother.

Tea Bag Loss

This is a newer superstition, but if the tag comes off while the tea bag is in the cup, it is said to indicate that the person will lose something within the week.

Chapter Eleven

Tea Etiquette

Etiquette requires us to admire the human race.

Mark Twain (1835–1910)

TEA ETIQUETTE HARKENS BACK TO DAYS GONE BY, WHEN conventions and social conventions were much more rigid. Not surprisingly, most of the standard tea etiquette dates back to the days of the British Empire.

In the Regency and Victorian eras, social etiquette reached fastidious proportions, and virtually every activity had its own expected code of etiquette. Children were versed in social etiquette at a very early age in the nineteenth century. They were taught how they should behave in all manners of social situations: how they should greet people; how they should walk, talk, carry, and wear things. Table etiquette was considered of inestimable importance. Since tea had become such an integral part of society by the Victorian era, it acquired an entire array of manners and customs that were supposed to show that one was a person of good breeding.

You may very well think that all that is just tea snobbery. Perhaps it is, yet there is no excuse for rudeness, and it doesn't cost anything to be polite. It is worth knowing, therefore, a bit about the etiquette of tea for the next time you drink it at the Ritz or when you are invited to drop in to see the Queen of England. You never know! And you wouldn't want her to think you are a commoner, would you?

Social Divisions Linked by a Drink

Tea etiquette was originally built up around meals, for tea was the favored drink in Britain with every meal. Nowadays, we tend to think of polite afternoon tea as being the occasion when pinkies need to be raised, cucumber sandwiches are placed delicately on plates, and tea is poured in a ritualized manner. But afternoon tea was a meal that was introduced relatively late in society. And it wasn't at all the same as high tea, with which it is often mistaken. In fact, the two were quite distinct meals and the thing that divided them was class!

British society was structured in three classes: the nobility and landed gentry, who were regarded as upper class; the middle classes, who included the office professions and clerical occupations; and the working class, who were regarded as lower class. England in the eighteenth century was no place to be if you were poor, and it was not a whole lot better at the start of the nineteenth century. This is not meant to be a diatribe about the English class system but rather a statement that society was grossly unequal in terms of what possessions and income people had. There were huge differences in both how individuals spent their time and in the different types of food that they ate. Indeed, this led to the classes having a different set of meals. The only thing that united them was tea.

How the Meals Changed

In the eighteenth century, meals were served in wealthy families at breakfast, then dinner was at four in the afternoon, followed by supper in the evening. Gradually these times changed as the century progressed, with breakfast starting at 10:00 AM and dinner moved back later to take the place of supper. As this happened, a new meal was introduced, called lunch. As dinner became later in the evening, and the gap between dinner and lunch grew, people started to get hungry in the afternoon.

This long gap proved too much for one of Queen Victoria's ladies in waiting, Anna, the seventh Duchess of Bedford. She started to have her servants serve her tea and cakes in her boudoir during these times between lunch and dinner. Other ladies soon followed suit, and eventually everyone in her circle was taking tea in the afternoon. Thus afternoon tea was invented, and it grew to include tea, savory pastries, thinly cut sandwiches, biscuits, and cakes being served.

As the century progressed, ladies came out of the boudoirs and served afternoon tea in their drawing rooms, and gentlemen were often invited to drink with them. Afternoon tea became a social engagement wherein ladies would send out invitations announcing that they were "at home." People were expected to attend, and it was considered a social taboo not to reply "with regrets" if unable to attend. At these "at home" occasions, of which there would be one each day so that people could fill their calendar with a different afternoon tea every day of the week, the hostess would serve tea, sandwiches, cakes, and other snacks and would also have some sort of entertainment for her guests.

The working class, however, had no such leisure. In early Victorian England, even children were employed in factories, went down mines and up chimneys, and worked long hours. A series of social reforms gradually restricted the number of hours that women and children could work, but it was not until the Factory Act of 1878 that children under the age of ten were prohibited from working at all.

Breakfast for the working class consisted of bread and butter, with perhaps some thin gruel and a cup of tea. Dinner was a middle-of-the-day meal with the long working day supper serving as the main meal at the end of the day. It became known as high tea, as distinct from the afternoon tea of the upper and middle classes. To this day, families either refer to the evening meal as "tea" or "supper."

High tea is actually more of a meal than afternoon tea. It usually begins with a savory snack, like cheese on toast, scrambled eggs, or cold meats. Then follows toasted crumpets, pickles, scones, cakes, and a tea loaf. And, of course, there are copious amounts of black, milky tea.

Afternoon Tea Etiquette

The following are some of the dos and don'ts for when you are serving tea in the traditional afternoon fashion.

If you are "being mother":

- Pour milk into the cups of those who want it;
- Offer sugar cubes rather than a bowl of granulated sugar; and
- Use tongs to lift the cubes.

When you take your tea:

- When stirring a cup, do not rattle the spoon in the cup. No one should hear the spoon in the cup.
- After stirring, place the spoon behind the cup and to the right of the handle.
- Always remove the spoon from the cup before drinking.
- There is a myth that you should raise your pinkie finger when drinking tea. In fact, the correct way to hold the teacup is with the right index finger through the handle and the top of the handle steadied by placing the thumb on top and the bottom of the handle, which is supported by the middle finger. The fourth and pinkie fingers naturally bend inwards in the direction of the wrist.
- Sip the tea, and do not gulp. Remember that it is a hot drink and that you could burn your mouth.
- If the tea is too hot, then wait and allow it to cool. Do not blow on it; that is neither hygienic nor polite.
- Do not keep the teacup in your hand when not sipping. Place it back on the saucer.
- Never hold the cup with the palm of the hand or any other way than by using the handle. It will appear uncouth.

When you eat:

- Begin with the napkin. Unroll it and place it on your lap. It should not be tucked into your shirt or blouse. Once it has left the table, the napkin is not supposed to return to the table until you have finished your meal; so if you have to leave the table for a moment or two, it should be placed on the seat, not on the table. When you finish, place the napkin to the left of the plate.

- The fork is supposed to be used with the left hand and the knife with the right, if you decide to use them at all. It is not appropriate to use the fork with the right hand, unless you have a physical problem with the left hand. You don't have to use them since these are delicate little treats, so it is considered appropriate to use your fingers.
- Before eating scones, place a spoonful of jam and a spoonful of cream on your plate. Then you can split your scone.
- Be delicate in your eating. Don't gobble food, don't talk with your mouth full, and don't drink until you have swallowed your food.

Having said all that, in the next chapter we will look at what sort of fare you can serve or eat with your afternoon tea.

Chapter Twelve

Afternoon Tea

Stands the Church clock at ten to three? And is there honey still for tea?

Rupert Brooke, "The Old Vicarage," Grantchester, 1912

Afternoon tea should be provided, fresh supplies, with thin bread-and-butter, fancy pastries, cakes, etc., being brought in as other guests arrive.

Isabella Beeton (1836–1865), Mrs. Beeton's Book of Household Management

Another novelty is the tea-party, an extraordinary meal in that, being offered to persons that have already dined well, it supposes neither appetite nor thirst, and has no object but distraction, no basis but delicate enjoyment.

Jean-Anthelme Brillat-Savarin (1755–1826), The Physiology of Taste

THE CUSTOM OF HAVING "AT HOME" AFTERNOONS HAS long since gone, but you can still partake of formal afternoon tea at many fancy hotels. There, the etiquette that we looked at in the last chapter is appreciated, but of course, there is no way that it can be enforced.

Having your own afternoon tea can be enjoyable as well, serving it at whatever time you like between three and five o'clock in the afternoon, as this is the traditional time.

Serving Afternoon Tea

To prepare for your afternoon tea gathering, bring out your best, most delicate china tea set. Get out your cutlery and make sure it is gleaming. If it is silver, then consider the silver-cleaning experiment in chapter 15 to help it shine. Set the table with a linen tablecloth, and if you have one, place a white lace one on top. Place napkins to the left of each table setting.

Have everything needed to prepare your tea and have two teapots for the middle of the table, one for tea and one for hot water. To do it properly, use loose-leaf tea rather than tea bags. Of course, this means that you will also need a tea strainer and an accompanying pot to rest it on to catch any drops.

Milk should be served in a china jug, and the sugar cubes should be in a matching bowl. A small saucer or plate should be placed on the table for slices of lemon with cocktail sticks or a small fork to pick them up with.

The centerpiece should be a three-layered cake stand. Put paper doilies on each layer before adding the delicacies. Add the following on the various cake stand:

- Bottom layer—finger sandwiches (both white and brown/whole meal/granary bread) cut into triangles without crusts (e.g., smoked salmon, cucumber, egg with mustard and cress, cream cheese, ham)
- Middle layer—scones, muffins, or hot buttered toast, cut into small triangles
- Top layer—assorted cakes, a tea loaf, a fruit loaf, and fairy cakes

Place pots of clotted cream and jam for the scones on the table, perhaps with a honey pot and a dish with pats of butter.

High Tea

I am from Scotland and grew up with the tradition of Scottish High Tea. This is basically the same as the afternoon tea above, with the addition of a main course, which could be porridge, scrambled eggs on toast, bacon and eggs, or an omelet. One would serve this and then dine on the scones and clotted cream.

Some Recipes for Afternoon Tea

Homemade Bread

The following is a basic bread recipe that you can adapt for white or whole wheat bread. As it is described, it is for a white loaf, which you should find is excellent for cutting into thin slices for your sandwiches. Or, by changing the flour to half strong white flour and half whole meal or granary (I use a simple seeded flour to produce a pleasant white seeded bread—half strong white and half seeded flour), you can get the type of bread you wish. The technique remains the same.

REQUIREMENTS TO MAKE ONE LOAF

2 cups (1 pound) white plain flour (make sure that it is plain. Do *not* use self-raising flour, which is made up of plain flour, salt, and baking powder as a leavening agent)

2 teaspoons salt (or less)

2 teaspoons sugar

1 ounce (25 grams) fresh yeast

1 cup (½ pint) hand-hot water

1–3 tablespoons olive oil (optional)

METHOD

In a pitcher, mix the yeast and the sugar with a wooden spoon. This will quickly form a paste. Then add half of the water and stir this up. Sprinkle a pinch of flour over the surface of the liquid and then put this somewhere warm to rise. The mixture will gradually foam as the yeast ferments.

Meanwhile, put the flour and salt in a large bowl. Add the olive oil and stir it well. Put this somewhere warm as well.

Once the yeast mix has formed a foam head about two inches thick, it is ready to add to the flour.

Form a well in the middle of the flour and pour the yeast mix in. Then stir it well. Gradually add the rest of the water, stirring all the time. You are aiming to get a consistency that will let you form a ball. This needs a bit of experimenting, but you will gradually get it right. If you have added too much water, then you can add a little more flour. (In general, though, it is better to have less fluid than needed to begin with and gradually add more. You will find that if you start with too much fluid, then even adding more flour will not result in as firm a dough as you will with less fluid to begin with.)

Knead the dough. When it is well formed, take it out and on a lightly floured working surface knead it for about 8 to 10 minutes. Kneading means folding the dough over and over again, each time stretching and pressing it. You will find that it changes texture as you do so and becomes quite elastic.

Put the dough back in the bowl and cover it with a damp cloth. Put it somewhere warm again and allow it to rise for about an hour, to double its size. Knead the dough again so that it goes back to its original size. Work it into a sausage shape and place on a baking tray that you have greased with a pat of butter. Cover it with the cloth again and put it on a cool surface for a couple of hours. It will rise again. Once it has done so, make about three cuts on the top of the dough (this is so that it does not burst as it rises in the oven).

Preheat the oven to 350 degrees Fahrenheit (175 degrees Centigrade) and with oven gloves put the baking tray with the dough roll into the oven on the middle rung and leave it there for 35 to 40 minutes. Just keep an eye on it.

It should turn a beautiful golden color. When you take it out turn it upside down (again with oven gloves). It should sound hollow in the middle if you tap it. If it doesn't sound hollow, it is not ready.

You can give your bread a tea flavor by simply using an infused tea for the half pint of warmed water.

Scones

Here is a very simple recipe for afternoon tea scones:

REQUIREMENTS TO MAKE 12 TO 14 SCONES

¾ cup (200 ml) milk

1 ⅓ tablespoons (20 grams) butter

1 ¾ cups (400 grams) flour

1 pinch of salt

2 teaspoons of baking powder

METHOD

Warm the milk and the butter.

Mix the flour, salt, and baking powder together, then stir in the warm milk and butter and make a dough.

Grease a baking tray. Divide the dough and make each scone about 1 ½ to 2 inches (4 to 5 centimeters) in diameter with a cutter or just shape with your hands. Set the scones on the tray and bake in the oven at 325 degrees Fahrenheit (160 degrees Centigrade) for 15 to 20 minutes.

You can add raisins to the mixture and/or any spices that you wish.

Tea Loaf

This is a good basic tea loaf recipe that is tried and tested. It will produce a good tea loaf, which anyone can do, regardless of his previous baking experience. You can make the loaf taste of whatever tea you wish. The secret is just to make the tea very strong when you prepare the first stage overnight.

REQUIREMENTS TO MAKE A TEA LOAF

2 cups (1 lb) mixed dried fruit—currants, raisins, and sultanas

1 cup (8 oz) soft brown sugar

1 cup (½ pint) hot strong tea (Earl Grey, Darjeeling, or whatever type you prefer, but generally a black tea)

1 ½ cups (12 oz) self-rising flour (no yeast this time, since the self-raising flour contains the raising agent)

2 eggs

A small pat of butter to grease the bottom of the baking pan

EQUIPMENT:

One 2-lb loaf tin

Greaseproof paper

One large bowl and one small bowl

Spoon to stir

Cake tester

You can use either an ordinary oven or a fan-assisted oven to make this tea loaf.

STAGE ONE:

Mix the dried fruit, the tea, and the sugar in a large bowl, stir, then cover with seran wrap or a muslin towel and leave overnight to soak.

STAGE TWO:

Grease the loaf tin and line it with the greaseproof paper, leaving a collar of about an inch above the loaf tin. This will prevent the sides of the tea loaf from burning.

STAGE THREE:

Beat the eggs. Add the flour and eggs to the tea, fruit, and sugar mixture. Stir well and then pour the mix into the loaf tin.

Bake at 300 degrees Fahrenheit (150 degrees Centigrade) for 1¾ hours. If you use a fan-assisted oven the time may be slightly less.

Test with the cake tester wire. Push it right to the bottom and withdraw. If it is dry and there is no stickiness, the tea loaf is ready.

Remove the loaf from the oven and leave for five minutes. Then gently lift the loaf out by pulling the paper and it will come away nicely. Then gently peel the paper back and lift the tea loaf off and place on a rack to cool.

Once cool, the loaf is ready to slice, or it can be wrapped and placed in a pan to be ready for your afternoon tea.

Earl Grey Fairy Cakes with Honey and Frosting

These little fairy cakes made with Earl Grey tea have a pleasant bergamot flavor, and the peppery look of the cakes makes for a pleasing appearance as they are eaten.

This recipe will be enough to make ten fairy cakes.

INGREDIENTS:

⅔ cup (150 grams) self-rising flour

½ cup (110 grams) caster sugar

6 tablespoons (90 grams) butter

2 eggs

2 teaspoons of baking powder

4 tablespoons of milk

10 Earl Grey tea bags

METHOD:

Soak 4 tea bags in the milk for 10 minutes and then squeeze out the milk. Mix all the other ingredients together.

Snip off the ends of the remaining six tea bags and pour the tea into the mix. Stir well. Spoon the mix into fairy cake cases, two-thirds full.

Bake at 350 degrees Fahrenheit, or 325 if fan-assisted oven (175 and 160 degrees Centigrade, respectively) for 20 minutes.

THE FROSTING:

2 ⅔ tablespoons (40 grams) butter

½ cup (120 grams) mascarpone

2 tablespoons honey

1 ½ cups (340 grams) icing sugar

Mix all of the ingredients. Pipe or spread on the cooled fairy cakes, and enjoy your afternoon tea.

PART THREE

USING TEA

Chapter Thirteen

Tea Cocktails

My experience . . . convinced me that tea was better than brandy, and during the last six months in Africa I took no brandy, even when sick taking tea instead.

Theodore Roosevelt (1858–1919), Letter, 1912

THE ORIGIN OF THE WORD COCKTAIL IS UNCLEAR. THE first written reference to it in America was in the publication *The Farmer's Cabinet* on April 28, 1803. It includes a terse entry that describes a man drinking a cocktail, seemingly a medicinal one, then visiting the doctor, who seemed to be a wise man. Then the patient had another cocktail. But this is still speculation, as he doesn't describe what the concoction was actually made of.

A proper definition is given in Hudson, New York, in 1806, when the editor of *Balance and Columbian Repository* gave a true definition of a cocktail. He said that it was "a stimulating liquor, composed of spirits of any kind, sugar, water, and bitters." This seems to be the standard definition for what we now know as a cocktail. It is a mixed drink containing three or more ingredients, one of which must be a spirit of some kind.

There are many cocktails that have tea in their name, but that only pay lip service to tea, which is added as an afterthought. Some of them, like Tokyo Tea and Long Island Iced Tea, have many more than three ingredients and are quite alcoholic. Since this is a book about tea, the cocktails that are included here have tea as a main ingredient along with a spirit.

Some are variants of classics but with a tea twist, and others are new. Additionally, since tea was often advocated for instead of alcohol and was a steadfast part of the temperance movement of the nineteenth century, we will also look at some tea mocktails, or soft tea drinks.

Mixology

Mixology is the name given to the art (some would say the science) of mixing cocktails. But this is not just a matter of mixing a lot of ingredients together and hoping for the best. The essence of a mixologist's purposes is to mix appropriate flavors together to make a cohesive drink. The main flavors are strong, sweet, sour, and bitter. There are also smokiness and spiciness. A mixologist must determine how the flavors sit with one another and complement each other. When you think of which teas to add to cocktails, consider their flavors; for example, Assam is smoky, Darjeeling is floral and bitter, and Early Grey is abundantly floral and full of bergamot.

The following tea cocktails can be served in teacups (chilled beforehand) or can be served from a glass teapot into chilled teacups. And it's important to note that one measure equals one-half ounce.

Green Manhattan

The Manhattan was allegedly created in 1870, at the Manhattan Club in New York City at a banquet given by Lady Randolph Churchill in honor of the mayor, Samuel J. Tilden. Lady Randolph was the mother of Sir Winston Churchill. The inventor of the drink was Dr. Iain Marshall.

INGREDIENTS:

1 measure blended whiskey

½ measure of vermouth

1 dash Angostura bitters

1 measure infused and cooled green tea

Stir with cracked ice, then strain into a chilled teacup.

Mar-tea-ni

Traditionally, a Martini is a gin and vermouth cocktail garnished with an olive.

INGREDIENTS:

1 measure gin

⅓ measure vermouth

1 measure black tea

Stir in a glass with ice cubes, then strain into a chilled teacup. Squeeze a little lemon juice to lighten the drink. An olive is optional.

Hot Tea

This is a classic tea cocktail with an orange flavor.

INGREDIENTS:

1 measure of Cointreau

5 measures of black tea

A slice of orange

This is a hot tea cocktail, so use a heat-proof cup. Pour in the Cointreau first, then the hot tea, along with sugar if you need sweetness. Stir together, add a slice of orange, and allow to cool for comfort.

Saki-tea-me

This is a play on the old Rowan and Martin Laugh-In sketch show that ran from 1968 to 1973. "Sock it to me" was a catchphrase that led to the English actress Judy Carne receiving a dowsing with water. This drink bears no relationship to the dowsing, other than it is a play on the words, based around the ingredients: saki, green tea, and crème de menthe (the "me" for menthe).

INGREDIENTS:

½ measure saki

2 measures cooled green tea

1 measure crème de menthe

Crushed ice

Fill the cup with crushed ice, then pour in the saki and crème de menthe, then the cooled green tea. Stir well.

This has a very refreshing taste.

High Tea

Another classic cocktail with a tea base.

INGREDIENTS:

⅓ measure amaretto

⅓ measure Grand Marnier

5 measures hot black tea, sweetened

Mix the amaretto and the Grand Marnier in a heat-proof cup. Add the hot tea and stir well.

Mad Hatter's Tea

This is based on the well-known character in Lewis Carroll's *Alice's Adventures in Wonderland*. The Hatter was never actually referred to as mad by Carroll, but simply as The Hatter. The term "mad as a hatter" is thought to describe the symptoms of dementia that occurred in hat makers in the eighteenth and nineteenth centuries as a result of the mercury that the hat makers used in the production of felt.

This cocktail has no mercury in it and will not affect you in any way, other than to intoxicate you if too many are consumed. It refers to the episode in Carroll's book where The Hatter is stuck in a time loop and is forever uttering the words "Tea Time," causing people at his tea party to move around the table.

INGREDIENTS:

5 measures black tea

1 measure Frigola (which has a thyme flavor)

1 squeeze of lime to lighten the tea

Add the Frigola to a heat-proof cup and then add up to five measures of hot black tea. Add the lime juice a little at a time and watch the tea lighten.

Mocktails

The following recipes are for beverages with tea punches and tea variants without alcohol.

Angel Punch

A great, refreshing punch for a party of twenty people.

INGREDIENTS:

½ cup (125 grams) sugar

½ cup (4 fl oz) water

3 ¾ cups (900 ml) green or black tea

6 ½ cups (3 ¼ pints) white grape juice

Copious ice

6 ½ cups (3 ¼ pints) soda water

Boil the water and add the sugar to make a syrup. Mix with all the other ingredients except the ice and soda water. Keep cool in the fridge until ready and then add the ice and soda water.

Spice Tea

This is a good substitute for toddy. (A toddy is a mixed drink with a spirit, usually Scotch whisky, and sugar and spices. It is taken to fend off the cold.) Spice tea can be taken if you feel a cold coming on.

INGREDIENTS:

1 cup (250 ml) strong black tea

2 cloves

Zest of an orange (as much as your taste desires)

A teaspoon of honey

Add the tea to a cup, add the honey and cloves, and stir in the orange zest.

Mint Tea Punch

This recipes makes enough for four people.

INGREDIENTS:

2 ½ cups (600 mls) strong black tea

¾ cup (175 g) caster sugar

1 lemon, squeezed

1 ¼ cups (300 mls) orange juice

⅓ cup (75 grams) sliced strawberries (but make sure that no one has a strawberry allergy)

Half a sliced orange

Half a sliced lemon

Mint sprigs to garnish

Dissolve the sugar in the tea, then add the orange and lemon juice and put in the fridge to cool. It is ready once cooled through and just needs the garnish with the sliced fruit and mint.

A Healthy Sports Drink

This is a better drink for you after playing sports or working out than a soda.

INGREDIENTS

1 pot of green tea, freshly infused

2 teaspoons of honey

A dash of lemon juice

Add the honey to the tea in a jug and squeeze in the lemon juice. This can be taken as a warm drink or allowed to cool and taken later after a game or workout.

Iced Tea

We cannot leave this chapter without looking at iced tea, that very popular way of taking tea in the United States.

Straight Iced Tea

INGREDIENTS

4 tea bags

1 cup of sugar

Mint for garnish

Ice

Make your brew of tea with 4 tea bags of whatever type of tea you wish to use, in 4 cups of boiled water. Allow this to brew for 5 minutes and then remove the tea bags.

Take a jug and add a cup of sugar (or less according to taste) and 4 cups of cold water. Stir the sugar until dissolved. Then pour in the tea brew and mix. If you do it this way the final drink is less likely to be cloudy.

Then chill it in the fridge for 2 hours. When ready over ice pour into glasses and add mint to garnish.

Lemon Iced Tea

This is delicious and very popular. To make this, follow the above recipe, but simply add ¼ cup (60 ml) squeezed lemon juice. Adjust the sugar according to your taste.

Peach Iced Tea

INGREDIENTS

As above for Iced Tea

2 peeled and chopped peaches.

This is also done with the same recipe as above, but start it with the chopped peaches in the pot or a jug with the 4 tea bags. Allow to brew for 5 minutes, then remove the tea bags. You can either leave the peaches in and serve or remove them from the chilled jug just before serving.

Chapter Fourteen

The Health Benefits of Tea

Drinking a daily cup of tea will surely starve the apothecary.

Chinese Proverb

Tea tempers the spirits and harmonizes the mind, dispels lassitude and relieves fatigue, awakens thought and prevents drowsiness, lightens or refreshes the body, and clears the perceptive faculties.

Confucius (551–496 BC)

Tea is the elixir of life.

Lao Tzu (c. six century BC)

Sir, I did not count your glasses of wine, why should you number up my cups of tea?

Samuel Johnson (1709–1784), The Life of Samuel Johnson, Vol. 1

TEA WAS ORIGINALLY REGARDED AS A MEDICINAL DRINK. Legend has it that in the year 2737 BC, Emperor Shen Nong discovered tea and proclaimed that it would cure seventy types of poisons and several diseases. Over the millennia the benefits of tea as a drink have continuously been extolled, but it is fair to say that due to its ubiquity as a drink, the belief that tea has any real medical benefit has most likely been diluted over the years. A similar phenomenon occurred with aspirin, a common painkiller that was, for a time, considered by many people—doctors included—as nothing more than a sometimes-useful household remedy. Modern research, however, has demonstrated that this is far from the case. Aspirin is actually one of the most powerful and useful drugs known to modern medicine. It can reduce the risk of stroke, heart disease, and most types of cancer. And it does so by virtue of a single seemingly insignificant chemical group that modifies salicylic acid into acetyl-salicylic acid, or aspirin.

But what does aspirin have to do with tea? Tea, in all its varieties, actually does seem to have definite beneficial effects upon health, just like aspirin. And research over the past three decades continues to give us more insight into how this incredible drink can be helpful medicinally. Tea seems to protect our bodies against heart disease, strokes, and cancer, as well as other conditions like glaucoma, Alzheimer's disease, and even erectile dysfunction.

But first a word of caution: Science teaches us that things are never black or white. There may be great benefits from drinking tea, yet not all studies show the same benefits. Similarly, if a substance or medicine has such great benefit to our health, then it undoubtedly will produce this effect through a biochemical or pharmacological effect. That being the case, it is highly probable that some proportion of the people taking tea medicinally will react to it in an adverse way. This is also the case with aspirin and other drugs. So while a majority of people can take tea with no problem, a significant number will develop side effects. We must keep this in mind as we assess the benefits of tea as a medicinal drug. Too much of a good thing can lead to adverse side effects, so this must be applied to taking tea as a supplement as well.

The Different Types of Tea and Their Health Benefits

We have seen in chapter 7 that tea all comes from one plant, *Camellia sinensis*, and that the different types are the result of the way the tea leaves are processed. The following benefits of certain teas are simply a small representation of the ways in which tea could be beneficial to your health and wellness.

Green tea is shown to:

- Promote weight loss
- Reduce hardening of the arteries
- Lower cholesterol
- Reduce risk of Alzheimer's disease
- Reduce risk of Parkinson's disease
- Reduce risk of stroke
- Reduce risk of heart disease
- Interfere with growth of cancers of the bladder, breast, colon, stomach, pancreas, and lung

Black tea is shown to:

- Slightly reduce the harmful effects of cigarette smoke in the lungs
- Reduce the risk of stroke
- Reduce the risk of death after heart attack

White tea is shown to:

- Be protective against cancer (it appears this is the best tea for this)
- Reduce the risk of stroke
- Reduce the risk of heart disease

Oolong tea is shown to:

- Reduce weight
- Lower cholesterol

Pu-erh tea is shown to:

- Lower cholesterol

These benefits all come from positive studies of the health benefits of tea, but it is important to note that not all researchers have shown the same results, so at best they are simply suggested benefits.

The Chemistry of Tea

In order to better comprehend how some of these benefits from tea may arise, it is important to have an understanding of the basic chemistry of tea and of how the different processing of the leaves affects its chemistry. There are, in fact, thousands of different chemical molecules in tea leaves, and they have not all been identified.

The main chemical constituents of the tea leaves are polyphenols, alkaloids, carbohydrates, amino acids, various volatile chemicals (which impart flavor and taste), aluminum, and various trace minerals and elements, including fluoride. The following are the most important chemicals for our understanding of tea's medicinal benefits.

Polyphenols

Polyphenols are chemicals produced in plants that help the plant defend itself from ultraviolet radiation, pathogens, and herbivorous creatures. These are the main chemicals that are thought to provide most of the health benefits in tea.

Over eight thousand polyphenols have been found in various plant species. They are known as secondary metabolites, which arise from phenylalanine, or shikimic acid. Polyphenols are classified according to the number of phenolic rings that they possess. A basic phenol looks like this:

FLAVONOIDS

Flavonoids are the group of polyphenols that have been most studied. They all have a similar chemical structure, consisting of three rings:

More than four thousand different flavonoids have been identified, and they fit into six groups:

- Flavones (luteonin, apigenin, tangeritin)

- Flavonols (quercetin, kaemferol, myricetin, isorhamnetin, pachypodol)

- Flavanones (hesteretin, naringenin, eriodictyol)

- Catechins or flavanols

- Anthocyanidins (cyanidin, delphinidin, malvidin, pelargonidin, peonidin, petunidin)

- Isoflavones (genistein, daidzein, glycitein)

Generally, flavonoids are used for multiple purposes in plants. They work within the plant as hormones, ultraviolet light defenders, metabolic controllers, and protectors against fungi, bacteria, and insects. Flavonoids are the most important plant pigments, giving flowers color to attract insects for pollination and making fruits attractive to birds and animals, including humans!

Alkaloids

Alkaloids are chemicals that contain carbon, hydrogen, and nitrogen atoms. Some also contain sulfur, oxygen, chlorine, bromine, and phosphorus. Alkaloids often have drug-like effects, and indeed, alkaloids are what make herbal remedies useful. Many drugs obtained from plants are derived from the various alkaloids.

The main alkaloids in tea are all stimulants and include:

- Caffeine ($C_8H_{10}N_4O_2$)

- Theobromine ($C_7H_8N_4O_2$)

- Theophylline ($C_7H_8N_4O_2$)

(Note that theobromine and theophylline have the same chemical formula but different structures.)

Vitamins and Minerals

Tea's main vitamin is C, though green and oolong teas contain more vitamin C than black tea. There are also smaller amounts of vitamins B1, B2, K, E, niacin, and folic acid in tea that can be beneficial to our health.

Tea also contains small amounts of the minerals manganese, potassium, and fluoride.

Catechins: The Key Players

Catechins are one of the main types of flavonoids. They are important secondary metabolites. This means that they are involved in the defense system of the plant, as opposed to primary metabolites, which are involved in the processes of growth, development, and reproduction. Their ability to defend the plant against animals or insects that would otherwise eat or damage the plants is actually what makes them so beneficial when humans drink catechin-rich tea.

Fresh tea leaves contain four main catechins. Thus green and yellow tea, both of which have not gone through the oxidation process (they are unfermented teas) are as close as one can get to the natural chemicals. The following four natural chemicals seem to produce most of the health benefits. These chemicals are as follows:

- Epicatechin (EC ($C_{15}H_{14}O_6$))

- Epicatechin galate (ECg ($C_{22}H_{18}O_{10}$))

- Epigallocatechin (EGC ($C_{15}H_{14}O_7$))

- Epigallicatechin gallate (EGCG ($C_{22}H_{18}O_{11}$))

The beauty of these chemicals is that they are powerful antioxidants. Antioxidants are natural chemicals that are involved in the prevention of cell damage, which is the common pathway for inflammation, aging, and a whole host of degenerative diseases. Antioxidants are preventative as they mop up free radicals, which are the culprits that cause a slew of problems for humans.

In many metabolic processes, where a chemical reaction called oxidation takes place, free radicals are produced. These are atoms or groups of atoms with an odd number of unpaired electrons. Free radicals are very reactive and can start a type of chain reaction, in the way that rows of dominos tumble into one another. The end result is damage to cell components, such as the DNA and the cell membranes. It is similar to leaving a rubber band exposed to the air for a long time: it becomes brittle and frayed. That is similar to what happens to a cell membrane when a free radical gets attached to it. Free radicals can also damage the lining of blood vessels and compromise the integrity of any tissue or organ in the body.

Epigallicatechin gallate (EGCG) is the most abundant of these catechins and has been the subject of a great deal of research into its health benefits. It is one of the most studied antixodants.

How Much Goodness Is In a Cup of Tea?

"Goodness" here refers to how many antioxidants are in tea, and there are quite a lot. If you make a cup of tea with ¼ teaspoon (1 gram) tea in ½ cup (100 ml) water, brewed for 3 minutes, this will yield 250 to 350 milligrams of tea solids which 40 percent are catechins and 6 percent are caffeine and alkaloids.

Black tea does not have as many antioxidants, because of the oxidation that takes place during the leaves' processing. This comes about as the leaves are cut and bruised, wherein the cell juices in the leaf are released together with the enzymes polyphenol oxidase and peroxidase. These enzymes break down many of the catechins into two compounds:

theaflavin and thearubigin, which are also antioxidants but seem to be less effective than the catechins.

Thearubigin gives black tea its dark color and its body. Theaflavin gives a brisk and bright taste to tea.

After oxidation has taken place, black tea only has 5 to 10 percent catechins left, since the rest have been converted to theaflavin and thearubigin. This does not mean that black tea does not have health benefits. It certainly does, just not as much as green tea.

Research on Tea's Health Benefits

Although there has been a lot of research into the health benefits of tea, the verdict of tea's real benefits are still inconclusive. At best, it is suggestive that tea is beneficial in several areas, Certainly, the studies that have been done indicate that further research is both desirable and worth doing.

Generally, there are three types of research on the health benefits of tea:

1. *Laboratory studies*, in which actual chemistry is studied, or the effects of tea or its constituents are tried out on animals;
2. *Epidemiological studies*, (population studies) that measure outcomes and look at tea-drinking habits; and
3. *Clinical trials*, which means studies of actual patients in an attempt to see whether tea drinking has a benefit after a set time.

We will look at all types of research in relation to the areas that have been subjected to study. The references, for those who may wish to follow the actual scientific studies, may be found at the end of the book.

Tea and Cancer

Laboratory studies have shown that:

- Tea polyphenols may inhibit tumor cell growth and apoptosis both in the laboratory and in animal studies. [31,32] Apoptosis is the name that we give to the process of cell death.

- Catechins inhibit angiogenesis and also inhibit tumor cell tendency to spread.[33]
- Green tea activates various protective enzymes that help to protect against tumor formation.[34]
- Both green and black teas have been found to inhibit the growth of prostate cancer cells that were implanted into laboratory mice.
- Tea polyphenols have been shown to protect against damage by ultraviolet light.

Epidemiological studies on the benefits of tea in fighting or preventing cancer are as follows:

- In 1994, a Chinese study looked at over one thousand men and women who had developed cancer of the esophagus and matched them with a control group.[35] They were all interviewed and asked about an extensive number of factors, including alcohol, smoking, diet, and tea consumption. They concluded that there was a significant reduction of risk of developing cancer in those who drank green tea.
- In 2012, a study was published that followed 69,000 healthy women for over a decade. It was found that those who drank green tea three times a week had a 14 percent lower risk of developing cancer of the digestive tract than those who did not drink it at all.[36]
- There have been over fifty epidemiological studies on tea and cancer since 2006. Some of these studies have demonstrated a reduced risk of developing cancer of the colon, breast, lung, ovary, and prostate by drinking tea. The results, however, are not conclusive, since the trial design and differences in type of tea and the method of production may not have been rigorous enough to satisfy scientific standards.

There have been several clinical trials conducted on the usefulness of tea in fighting or preventing cancer, but again, these have some inconsistent results:

- In 1999, a study on leukoplakia, a premalignant mouth condition, found that taking green tea and applying tea products to the lesions resulted in significant reduction in the lesions in the tea drinkers.[37]

- In 2003, a study of heavy smokers concluded that those who drank green tea had a significantly reduced urinary excretion of a marker chemical that is associated with DNA damage and is an indicator of increased cancer risk.[38]

- In a 2006 study from the University of California in Los Angeles, the effect of green and black tea extracts were looked at in patients who had skin damage from radiotherapy for cancer. Researchers found that tea extracts reduced the duration of skin toxicity after radiotherapy by five to ten days. Green tea extracts were more effective than black tea extracts.

- In 2010, a Taiwanese study looked at the effect that green tea could have on reducing the risk of lung cancer in smokers. Researchers looked at 70 patients with lung cancer and 340 healthy controls. Among smokers, those who did not drink green tea had a five-fold increased risk of lung cancer compared to those who drank one or more cups a day.

Tea and Heart Disease

Research has shown the following correlations between drinking tea and reducing the risk of heart disease:

- In a 1976 study from the Medical College in Calcutta (modern day Kolkata), green tea was found to be protective against having a heart attack.

- In 2006, a study from Japan enrolled over forty thousand people and followed up with them over the course of eleven years.[39] Researchers found that people who drank more than five cups of green tea per day had a 16 percent lower risk of overall mortality, and in particular, a lower risk of heart disease, than people who drank less that a cup a day. The effects were better for women than men.

- In 2008, a study was performed at the Athens Medical School in which healthy volunteers had the diameter of their brachial artery (an artery in the arm) measured by ultrasound on three different occasions—after taking green tea, caffeine, or hot water.[40] Measurements were taken at 30, 90, and 120 minutes after imbibing the drinks. It was found that green tea significantly increased the dilation of the vessel, which was not found with either the caffeine or the hot water. This indicates that tea has a beneficial effect in dilating major blood vessels, which is not seen when a placebo (water) is taken. Further, the benefit is due to something other than the caffeine in the tea.

Other Health and Preventative Benefits from Tea

DIABETES

- A 2009 study from China looked at the polysaccharide levels of green, oolong, and black teas to see whether they could be useful in treating diabetes. Researchers found that the black tea polysaccharide had the most glucose-inhibiting effect.[41]
- In 2009, researchers in Switzerland looked at black tea consumption in fifty countries throughout the world and compared the consumption to the rates of diabetes and cancer, as well as to respiratory disease, cardiovascular disease, and infections in each country. Statistical analysis showed that diabetes rates were lower in countries with the highest levels of black tea consumption (Ireland, the United Kingdom, and Turkey).

GLAUCOMA AND OTHER EYE DISEASES

In a study of laboratory rats, a team in China looked at whether the catechin antioxidants in green tea could actually pass from the intestine to reach the tissues of the eye. They found that analysis of the eye tissues demonstrated that the retina (the "seeing" tissue at the back of the eye) and the aqueous humor (the fluid at the front of the eye) absorbed the individual catechins. Further to that, researchers discovered that green tea catechins reduced the oxidative stress in the eye for up to twenty hours after having green tea. The researchers suggest that regular green tea drinking could benefit the eyes.[42]

INFECTION CONTROL

Humans around the world face a problem with antibiotic resistance. Bacteria and other microbes are developing resistance to antibiotics because society has been demanding them and doctors have been prescribing them too widely. Effectively, we have been creating a toxic environment for the microbial world, and in turn, these bacteria have been adapting and evolving to live in an environment that has become toxic to them.

The problem is that humans have to become more creative in how we are going to deal with the superbugs of the future. Scientists around the world are looking at alternatives to antibiotics to fight these mutant bacteria. Two natural substances that possess great interest to scientists are honey and tea.

Since green tea is regularly consumed in Egypt, Egyptian scientists suspected that a lot of patients would drink green tea when they took antibiotics. They wanted to see whether the green tea interfered with the antibiotics. They tested green tea in combination with twenty-eight disease-causing microorganisms. In every case, the scientists found that green tea enhanced the bacteria-killing activity of the antibiotics. In some cases, the tea made the antibiotic three times more effective. And green tea also made 20 percent of drug resistant bacteria susceptible to one of the cephalosporin antibiotics.

PARKINSON'S DISEASE

An American study on laboratory-induced Parkinson's disease that was conducted in 2007 found that the polyphenols in green tea had a protective effect against the disease. Specifically, the green tea polyphenols seem to protect certain dopamine nerve cells. Parkinson's disease, a neurological condition characterized by slowness of movement, rigidity of muscles, and a shaking tendency, is a result of depletion of dopamine.

In 2000, a Hawaiian study of eight thousand men found that those who drank more than three cups of tea per day were five times less likely to develop Parkinson's disease than those who did not drink it.

CHOLESTEROL

Cholesterol is a type of waxy, fatty substance that is found in all of the cells of the body. It is an important substance but one that is only needed in moderation. Cholesterol is carried around the bloodstream in packets called lipoproteins. The *lipo* is the inside part of the package and consists of fat. The *protein* is the outer part. There are two types of lipoprotens that carry your cholesterol: low density liporotein, or LDL, commonly known as the bad cholesterol; and high density lipoprotein, or HDL, commonly thought of as good cholesterol.

The problem with too much LDL is that it tends to cause a buildup of cholesterol in your arteries. Imagine that the lining of an artery is like a sponge with lots of small holes in it. Think of LDL cholesterol as being like a small ball, about the size of the holes in the sponge. By contrast, HDL cholesterol is like a much bigger ball, much larger than the holes. So if you have blood carrying a mixture of both types of ball, a large proportion of the small balls will lodge themselves in the holes. The larger ones will just bounce off and continue on their way. That is how bad cholesterol affects your blood vessels.

Several studies on rats suggest that all types of tea have some cholesterol lowering abilities. In animals fed a high-fat diet, green tea, black tea, and tea polyphenols prevented the elevation of serum and liver lipids and decreased total cholesterol.[43]

WEIGHT LOSS

Oolong tea has a long reputation for helping people to stay slim or to lose weight. A lot of the evidence is anecdotal rather than scientific, however. A study published in the *American Journal of Clinical Nutrition* in 2005 is worth noting.[44] The study was done with thirty-eight men who were assigned to one of two groups. On group was asked to drink a bottle of oolong tea every day containing 22 miligrams of catechins. The other group was asked to drink a bottle of oolong tea a day containing 690 miligrams of catechins. After twelve weeks, the high catechin group showed a significant reduction in body mass index, waist circumference, and body-fat mass compared to the lower intake group.

The Wonder of Pu-erh Tea

At this point it seems appropriate to pay special attention to Pu-erh tea. As you will recall, Pu-erh tea is a post-fermented tea, and it has been found to have the ability to inhibit an enzyme called fatty acid synthase, or FAS. This enzyme appears to be involved in obesity and also in some types of cancer (FAS has been found in elevated levels in some forms of cancer). Pu-erh tea may have some anticancer effects, but more research will need to be done before it is conclusive.

In addition, Pu-erh tea has been studied for its cholesterol-lowering ability. At Kunming Medical College in China, a study was performed on eighty-six patients with very high cholesterol levels. Researchers randomized the patients into two groups: one half was given Pu-erh tea three times a day, and the other was given a standard effective cholesterol drug. After two months, both groups showed a 65 percent reduction in cholesterol. Interestingly, the Pu-erh tea group also showed a reduction in triglyceride levels.

Side Effects of Tea

There are several components of tea that can cause harmful side effects if taken in excess. These components include:

- Fluoride
- Tannins
- Alkaloids (caffeine, theobromine, and theophylline)
- Oxalates
- Vitamin K

Most people have no problem drinking tea, but some do react to it if they drink too much. And some people are very sensitive to tea and cannot drink it at all.

Fluoride

Fluoride can cause the well-known effect of browning of the teeth. One would have to drink a lot of tea to have this reaction, however. If you consume only six cups of tea per day, fear not. You should be at a low risk of too much fluoride.

Tannin

Tannin in tea can chelate to certain metals and minerals in the diet and prevent their absorption. This is a chemical term meaning that one substance binds to another. In particular, it can chemically bind with iron, so if you have a tendency towards anemia, then you should not drink tea with meals, since it will prevent the iron in your food from being absorbed. Consuming a fruit drink with your meal instead of tea will help your body to better absorb the iron. This is because vitamin C boosts iron absorption.

Animal Iron Is Better Absorbed Than Plant Iron

The iron in meat is in the form of "heme" iron, whereas the iron from plants is "non-heme." Tea tannins do not interfere with heme absorption, but they decidedly do with non-heme. The trouble is that heme iron is absorbed more efficiently than non-heme. Heme is absorbed at a rate of 10 to 30 percent, whereas non-heme is only absorbed at a rate of 2 to 10 percent. The reduction by tea tannins on this non-heme iron can be enough to produce anemia. So if you are vegetarian, it may be best to avoid tea at meal times.

The effect of too much tannin in the body can be to produce nausea. The addition of milk to tea tends to reduce the problems of tannins, because the milk binds to the tannin and reduces its effect. Tannins can also chelate calcium, so it is best not to drink too much tea around mealtimes if you are at risk for developing osteoporosis. Away from meal times is fine.

Osteoporosis

Osteoporosis is commonly known as "thinning of the bones." In osteoporosis, the Bone Mineral Density (BMD) is reduced as a result of loss of calcium so that the bone architecture is disrupted, the bones are less dense, and fractures are more likely. It is most common in post-menopausal women and is certainly the most common bone disorder in the elderly. Osteoporosis affects at least 20 percent of women by the age of seventy.

Caffeine

Caffeine is the alkaloid that has the most stimulant effect in tea, although theobromine and theophylline also contribute. Because of caffeine's stimulant effect, too much caffeine can cause:

- Nausea
- Palpitations
- Insomnia
- Frequency of urine passage, due to being a mild diuretic

Oxalates

Oxalates can crystallize in the urinary tract to cause kidney stones. The quantity of oxalates in tea is quite small, so you would have to drink excessive amounts of tea to produce this.

Vitamin K

Like all vitamins, vitamin K is needed by the body. Its function is to help blood to clot, so it can help the body to heal wounds. Vitamin K could potentially interfere with the action of anticoagulant drugs or aspirin. These drugs may be prescribed by a doctor in order to reduce the risk of having a blood clot, for example if there is a risk of having a heart attack or a stroke. If someone were taking these drugs then they should discuss with their own doctor whether they can have tea or not. Green tea has the highest levels of vitamin K of all teas.

Conclusions on the Health Benefits of Tea

As we have seen, there have been many studies that suggest that drinking tea is beneficial to our health. On that basis, you may feel that tea drinking may be a good and justified addition to your daily routine to help you keep healthy or to try to prevent illness. It would be an added reason to enjoy tea on a regular basis.

Chapter Fifteen

Fun with Some Quirky Tea Experiments

Eureka! I have found it!

Archimedes (287–212 BC)

IN THE LAST CHAPTER, WE LEARNED ABOUT THE SCIENCE of tea and its various properties. Now it's time to put that knowledge to work with some interesting experiments that you can do in your own kitchen or tea laboratory to confirm some of the properties of tea.

Caution!

While none of these experiments are hazardous, you should take precaution by always wearing goggles during an experiment, just as you would in a science lab. This is to ensure that you don't get any splashes of liquid in your eye or anything that could irritate or damage the eyes.

A Dramatic Experiment to Prove the Antioxidant Ability of Green Tea

As noted in the previous chapter, antioxidants are natural chemicals that are involved in the prevention of cell damage, which is the common pathway for inflammation, aging, and a whole host of degenerative diseases. Antioxidants do this by mopping up free radicals, which are the culprits that cause various problems.

For this experiment you will need:

- 3 glasses or jam jars
- 2 dessertspoons of rice
- A small cup of green tea
- A few drops of tincture of iodine

Method

Pour some boiled water over the rice in a jam jar and stir it up to get rice water. This is essentially a starch solution. (You can, if you wish, also use water that you have boiled potatoes in.) Add a few drops of iodine, which will make the solution turn inky blue. Mix it well so that it is completely blue or black.

Pour some of this solution into another jar and then add water; you will see that the color remains, but will be very dilute and thinner. In other words, simply diluting it will not get rid of the color.

Now add the small cup of green tea to the main jar with the inky blue rice water. All the inkiness will dramatically disappear, and you will be left with relatively clear rice water.

Explanation

Iodine is a strong oxidant that reacts with starch. The antioxidants in the green tea reduce the iodine to "iodides," which are colorless.

This experiment suggests that antioxidants can work fast and dramatically. In the body it takes time for the things we ingest to get into our system and to be distributed at the cellular level. The effects are not as swift as in this illustrative *in vitro*, or "test tube" experiment, but antioxidants do seem to have a beneficial effect. The results of this simple experiment may just be enough to convince you of the health benefits of drinking green tea.

Oxidation and Reduction

These are two types of chemical reactions that often occur simultaneously throughout nature. Oxidation and reduction reactions involve an electron exchange between chemical reactants. It can confuse a lot of people, so here is what you need to know in relation to tea:

- Oxidation occurs when a reactant loses electrons in the reaction.
- Reduction occurs when a reactant gains electrons.
- Oxidation is the main reaction that takes place in tea processing.
- Oxidizing reagents facilitate oxidation.
- Reducing agents facilitate reduction.
- In the body, oxidation reactions often produce free radicals, which are harmful.
- Antioxidants are reducing agents and they counteract oxidation.

Toasting Tea: The Genmaicha Experiment

During the Tang dynasty, the Chinese began preparing tea bricks. Part of the process involved toasting tea leaves. This imparted a toasted flavor to the final brew. Toasting involves complex chemical changes and is one of the means by which foods are browned.

The Maillard Reaction

The Maillard Reaction was first described by Louise-Camille Maillard in 1912, when he was trying to synthesize proteins. He discovered that a series of chemical reactions take place between sugars and the amino acids that make up some proteins when something is toasted. The molecules containing an amine group ($-NH_2$), typically an amino acid, meet a sugar molecule, like glucose, in the presence of heat. A water molecule is then eliminated, thereby forming a compound called a Schiff base. This rapidly changes into another compound called an Amadori product. This then reacts with other molecules to produce a variety of ring-like or cyclical aromatic molecules. These produce the tantalizing smell and flavor of cooked or toasted food.

This is an extremely complex process that may produce two or three hundred of these aromatic chemicals. The Maillard Reaction only takes place at high temperatures, however. That is why cooks use fats or oils to baste food or to fry them in, so they attain a high enough temperature at which they will brown.

Genmaicha

Genmaicha is the name given to a type of toasted green tea that is consumed in Japan. The tea is not actually toasted, but it is combined with toasted brown rice. It was originally consumed by poor people, since tea was costly but rice was cheap. Nowadays, it is enjoyed by people from all strata of Japanese society.

Interestingly, genmaicha is commonly called "popcorn tea," as in the toasting of the rice, lots of the grains will turn themselves inside out like popcorn.

To make your own genmaicha at home, you will need:

- A frying pan
- ¼ cup (2 ounces) brown rice
- A teapot with an infuser or a tea strainer
- A teacup
- Green tea leaves

Method

Heat the frying pan and then spread the brown rice over the bottom in a thin layer. Toast the rice for about five minutes, shaking the pan all the time. You will find that the rice will start to swell and gradually turn brown. Lots of grains will undergo a popcorn effect. The majority will puff up like puffed rice cereal. Judge how brown you want the grains. The darker they become, the more flavor will be produced as the Maillard Reaction occurs. Don't burn the rice, however, since that will give you a charcoal taste, which is unpleasant.

Once finished, remove from the heat and allow the grain to cool.

When you are ready to make your genmaicha, add about a tablespoon of the puffed brown rice to the infuser, along with your green tea leaves. This is enough for a small pot of tea. Add near-boiled water and allow the mixture to infuse for about three minutes. Then you are ready to drink it. You will find that this process produces a wonderful toasted tea flavor.

The Popcorn Effect

Interestingly, popcorn has been around for a long time. Apparently, archaeologists have found fragments of cooked popcorn in a New Mexico cave that have been carbon-dated and found to be four thousand years old. People in the Americas have been fascinated by the popcorn effect for centuries.

A corn kernel has three main parts consisting of the pericarp or husk, the starchy endosperm on the inside, and the germ, which becomes the corn plant. When you heat the corn kernel, the pericarp holds in the steam created when the endosperm, which is made up of 14.5 percent water, heats up. This happens incredibly quickly, the internal temperature rising to 350 degrees Fahrenheit (175 degrees Centigrade) and 135 pounds per square inch. The pericarp then pops, and the starch explodes. This is the popcorn effect. Those yellow stringy bits that get stuck between your teeth are the remnants of the pericarp, which effectively had been blown inside out.

The Crackle Effect

You will find the aroma that is produced by the toasted brown rice quite delightful. The product will look and taste rather like puffed rice breakfast cereal. You may even find that it is tastier. And being made from brown rice, it is a very healthy dish. If you wish, you can have a dish of this along with your genmaicha. Just add milk to it and enjoy the crackling effect that is so characteristic of puffed rice.

This crackle effect is universally known and has been used by cereal manufacturers as a sort of slogan. Why these puffed rice grains should make these noises, however, has not been clear until recently. Interestingly, it is related to the popcorn effect.

During the swelling of the rice grains as they are heated, lots of little channels and chambers are formed in the grain. The starch forms into a crystalline structure, like glass. When the grains are immersed in milk, they absorb it, which squeezes air into the chambers until a critical pressure is reached and they explode. That's right, they explode in the same way that glass will crack and explode when submitted to pressure.

An Extra Balloon Experiment

This is a neat little experiment you can do as you make your genmaicha.

You will need:

- 1 tablespoon of toasted brown rice
- A bottle of soda
- A balloon

Method

Use about a tablespoon of your toasted brown rice and drop it into a balloon. You may need a funnel to do this or simply fold a piece of paper into a funnel shape. Take a bottle of soda and open it. Now stretch the balloon over the mouth of the bottle and hold the balloon so that the rice falls into the liquid. Then just let the balloon flop down and watch. You will see that the toasted brown rice starts to fizz, enough to cause the balloon to slowly inflate.

Rice grains will sink, accumulate bubbles around them, and then rise, with the others following suit. They will keep this up for a while as the balloon continues to inflate.

Explanation

Each rice grain has already bubbled and formed chambers that will contain gas. As they soak up the water, their gas is released. This, together with the carbon dioxide that is released from the soda, will inflate the balloon.

Tea As a Natural Indicator

Indicators are chemicals used to differentiate between acids and alkalis. Humans have known about the presence of acids since 8000 BC. That sounds incredible, but archaeological evidence from the Middle East shows that vinegar was being used and stored in jars in those early days. The ancient Egyptians were using it as an antiseptic in the third millennium BC, and there is a legend that Queen Cleopatra once had a precious pearl necklace dissolved in vinegar so that she could prove that she could consume a fortune in a single meal. Essentially, an acid is a chemical that eats or erodes materials. Acids can also be used to preserve foods.

Alkalis were known to the ancient Greeks and are quite different from acids, having a slimy, soapy feel to them. Alkalis were found to be useful in cleaning things. Nowadays, we use them as detergents and bleaches.

Robert Boyle (1627–1691) was the first chemist, and he made count-less important scientific discoveries and wrote the first chemistry text-book, *The Skeptical Chymist*, in 1661. Boyle was interested in acids and alkalis and wondered how one could differentiate them besides tasting them, which was potentially dangerous. He therefore turned his atten-tion to the work of French dyers who used various plant juices to dye silks. Boyle discovered that purple plant juices were turned red by acids, whereas alkalis turned them bluish-green. Thus, Boyle discovered the principle of indicators.

One of Boyle's great inventions was litmus paper, which is used in every school lab to this day. Boyle soaked paper in lichen juice and dried it to produce purple paper. When dipped in acid it turns red, and when dipped in an alkali solution, it turns blue. Nowadays, we use blue litmus paper to test for acids, which turn it red. And we use red litmus paper to test for alkalis, which make it turn blue.

There are several plant chemicals that are natural indicators, and tea is one of them. For this experiment on indicators, you'll need:

- 3 small glasses or jars
- A pot of cold black tea
- A lemon
- A pinch of sodium bicarbonate or baking soda

Method

Brew your tea and allow it to cool. Pour a couple of inches into each jar or glass. (Incidentally, if pouring a hot liquid into a glass, it is ideal to put a spoon into the glass. This will stop the glass from cracking, since the heat will be conducted up the spoon.)

Squeeze your lemon into the first glass. You will note that the liquid immediately turns much lighter than the middle jar. Then drop the pinch of sodium bicarbonate into the last glass. It will immediately turn very dark.

You can, of course, drink the tea with lemon, but the one with bicar-bonate will taste terrible.

Explanation

The anthocyanins in the tea are color-changing pigments that respond to changes in the tea's pH, which measures the range of acidity or alkalinity in a solution. (An anthocyanin is a derivative of an anthocyanidin when it has been coupled with a sugar.)

Black Tea—The Metal Detector

You can use tea to check food for iron content in this rather neat little kitchen experiment. For this experiment, you will need:

- A few jars or test tubes (as many as the foods you plan to study)
- A blender (or failing that a good fork to mash the food up)
- Some coffee filters
- A good strong pot of black tea made from 5 or 6 tea bags

Method

Brew a pot of strong tea and allow it to cool. It needs to be as strong as possible.

Now prepare the food that you want to test. Put it in the blender or macerate it with a fork. Add a little water in order to make a puree. Once it is fluid enough, filter it through the coffee filter into a jar or test tube.

Gradually add tea and gently stir.

If there is iron in the food, you will start to see a black precipitate begin to form.

Allow the mixture to settle for about five minutes, then filter through a fresh coffee filter. You have now extracted the iron from the liquid.

Explanation

The tannins in the tea will chelate, or chemically bind, to the iron and the iron gets thrown down as a precipitate. This is iron tannate.

People often imagine that tannins relate to tannic acid, which is used to tan leather. There is, however, no tannic acid in tea. The tannins are actually catechins, which we considered in chapter 8, together with other bioflavonoids.

Chelation is the name for a process by which certain ions and molecules chemically bind to metal ions. Iron is easily chelated by tea tannins, but so too are other metals like copper.

Einstein's Tea Leaves

Albert Einstein apparently liked a good cup of tea. It intrigued him, however, that when a cup of tea was stirred, the tea leaves always collected in the center of the bottom of the cup. Genius that he was, he set about working out why this happened.

But what is so fascinating about tea leaves collecting in the bottom of the cup? If you consider centrifugal force, you might conclude that the leaves would be thrown outward toward the sides of the cup when stirred. The tea leaf paradox, however, is one of those strange little effects that is contrary to one's expectation. In 1926, Einstein worked out that that friction at the bottom of the cup suppresses the outward force and causes an opposing force that pushes the tea leaves toward the center. You can test this out at home with any cup of tea with leaf debris at the bottom.

Clean Your Silver Teaspoons the Scientific Way

The following is a good way to keep your silver teaspoons clean—and any other silver you use to make tea. This cleaning method is fast and effective, and it takes all of the labor out of the process.

You will need:

- A bowl or basin
- A sheet of aluminum foil
- 1 tablespoon of sodium bicarbonate or baking soda
- The silver things you want to clean

Method

Take the bowl or basin and cover the bottom with aluminum foil, bending the edges up to make a sort of foil tray. It works best if the foil is a bit crinkly. Then sprinkle a thin layer of baking soda on the tray. Lay the silver objects that you want to clean on the bottom. Next, pour very hot water over to cover the objects.

You will soon see bubbles start to form almost immediately, and a rotten egg smell will be produced. As you watch, the silver will start to become clean, wherever it has been in contact with the aluminum. If parts are not in contact, then turn them so they are and the process of cleaning will continue (be careful when turning these pieces as the water will be very hot!). You will only need to soak the pieces for a few minutes and then they should be clean. Remove the objects and rinse them. You will see that a dark residue has formed on the aluminum foil. Dispose of the aluminum foil once finished.

Explanation

This cleaning effect happens due to an electrochemical reaction. When silver is exposed to the air, it reacts with sulphur substances that produce a tarnish of silver sulphide. The baking soda produces an alkaline solution. This creates the right condition for the sulphur in the tarnish to react with the aluminum to form aluminum sulphide (the dark residue that is left), leaving the silver free of tarnish. The sulphide has a greater attraction to the aluminum than it does to the silver. The slight rotten egg smell is characteristic of sulphides.

The Protective Effects of Tea Enzymes

This next experiment shows a very important protective chemical reaction that virtually every living organism has to be able to do and that is found in tea as well. For this experiment you'll need:

- A couple of small jars or test tubes
- A green tea bag
- A black tea bag
- Hydrogen peroxide (H_2O_2). This is obtainable from the drug store, usually in 3 percent solution. Be careful with this as it can bleach

surfaces if spilled. Always wash it off your hands should you come in contact with it.

Method

Snip the tea bags open and pour a good pinch into your jar or test tube. Do this for both the green and the black tea so that you have one container with green and one with black. Add about half an inch of hydrogen peroxide. Now watch.

You will start to see bubbles being formed that quickly rise to the surface. They will make the leaves rise and fall and will keep doing this for hours!

Explanation

These are bubbles of oxygen, which are produced by an enzymatic action to the hydrogen peroxide. The enzyme is called *catalase,* and it decomposes hydrogen peroxide into water and oxygen. This is an extremely important reaction in living cells. Hydrogen peroxide is produced as a toxic by-product in many metabolic processes. All living cells will produce some of it. All organisms that obtain their energy from the oxidation of food have had to develop a means of getting rid of it since it damages cells. This reaction is used to detect living cells, including bacteria, so it is very important.

The leaves in the tea bags consist of the fannings and broken leaves. This means that they have a very large surface-area-to-volume ratio, so they will infuse faster when you brew tea. This experiment shows that the enzyme will leach out rapidly, and the catalase will start to decompose the hydrogen peroxide into water and oxygen, both of which are safe to cells.

See Tea DNA

To conduct this experiment on tea's DNA, you'll need the following:

- One tea bag

- 1 ⅓ tablespoons (20 mls) colorless alcohol. You can use surgical spirit, gin, or vodka. This is best chilled
- 1 ⅓ tablespoons (20 mls) detergent
- A small cup or jar to mix in
- A coffee filter
- A pinch of salt
- A test tube or narrow jar

Method

Snip open the tea bag and put the tea in the jar. Add a little boiled water, about a dessertspoonful. Mix together to produce a slurry of tea. Add the salt and the detergent. Stir this up until you have a foamy, slimy tea mixture.

Filter the mixture through the coffee filter and collect the liquid in the test tube or the jar. You don't need very much of this liquid; an inch will do.

Next, take the chilled alcohol and tilt the test tube containing the filtered detergent/tea mixture very slightly. Then very carefully pour the alcohol down the side of the glass so that it forms a layer on top of the oily fluid. Then watch carefully. After a few seconds, a ghostly layer will start to form between the juice and the alcohol.

Congratulations! You have just extracted the DNA from *Camellia sinensis.*

(**NOTE**: Don't throw this away yet! There is another experiment you can try using this, after you have read the next section on topology.)

Explanation

As you mixed the tea together with the salt and the detergent, you broke down all the cellulose fibers that were holding the plant cells together so that they separated. This allowed the salt and the detergent to get to the cell walls where they attached themselves to the fatty acids in the cell membranes and caused them to burst open. As a result, the DNA from inside the cells leaked out into the fluid and dissolved in the water. When you added the alcohol, it precipitated the DNA out of the water as the white ring.

Now it is time to take a break from science and play a little game that you may remember from your childhood. It is a variant on cat's cradle. I want you to make a cup and saucer, and we'll use this to look at the mathematical subject of topology, which has a relevance to DNA

The Cup and Saucer: An Introduction to Topology

Many schoolchildren learn the string game called cat's cradle. This is how you make a string pattern called cup and saucer. You need a loop of string about thirty inches long. Simply follow these steps:

1. Hold your hands apart, palms facing. Loop the string over your thumbs and little fingers. This is the basic starting position.
2. Put your right index finger under the string that crosses your left palm and pull it back as you move your hands apart. The loop is now over the finger.
3. Repeat this move with the left index finger.
4. Loop the thumbs over the nearest of the index finger strings and under the farthest of the index finger strings.
5. Now you do a "navajo" with the thumbs. This means using your teeth to pull the lower of the thumb loops over the top of each thumb while retaining the higher one on the thumbs.
6. Now rotate the hands so that they are pointing away from you rather rather than pointing upward. Let the little finger loops free, and at the same time, pull your hands farther apart to tighten the string. You will see that you have a cup and saucer pattern.

Topology and Knot Theory

Topology is a major branch of mathematics, more specifically of geometry, that deals with connectedness and the way that basic properties are preserved under distortions of stretching and bending but not of tearing, cutting, or gluing. The way that the cat's cradle game can be distorted to produce the various string figures is of great interest to topologists.

Knot theory is a part of topology that is concerned with the study of mathematical knots. This has many applications, the least of them being the way that DNA behaves.

DNA is a double helix molecule that contains all of the genetic information about the life form it is extracted from. It is packed into a small area inside the nucleus of each cell. As two long strings that spiral around one another, DNA does occasionally become knotted. In order to replicate itself, which it has to do at each cell division, it must unknot itself. The way that it does this is through enzymatic action. The enzymes that do this are called *Topoisomerases,* and these incredible enzymes unwrap, unknot, and uncoil the DNA whenever it is needed.

That brings us back to the little precipitated ring that you produced in the last experiment. If you leave the ring for long enough, you will see that it has settled into a series of other fine rings that look very pretty. The tea topoisomerase enzymes are in one of those, ready and able to unknot one of the knottiest problems known to man, the DNA molecule.

So, as a rider to the DNA extraction experiment, you can add this little experiment. You will need:

- A bottle dropper with a bulb
- The test tube with the DNA extraction ring precipitate (see earlier experiment)
- 2 clean test tubes
- Hydrogen peroxide at 3 percent solution

Method

Use the bottle dropper to suck up the top layer above the ring. This is the alcohol layer. Put this into a clean test tube. Now suck up the ring precipitate and put it into the other clean test tube.

Add a little hydrogen peroxide to the first tube. You will get no reaction. Then add a little hydrogen peroxide to the second tube. You will get some effervescence (bubbling of oxygen).

Explanation

The precipitate contains catalase along with other enzymes, such as the topoisomerases that we have just talked about. The catalase releases oxygen, which is why you see the second tube bubbling.

Chapter Sixteen

Some Unexpected Uses of Tea

"Take some more tea," the March Hare said to Alice, very earnestly.

"I've had nothing yet," Alice replied in an offended tone, "so I can't take more."

"You mean you can't take less," said the Hatter: "it's very easy to take more than nothing."

"Nobody asked your opinion," said Alice.

Lewis Carroll (1832–1898), Alice in Wonderland

TEA NOT ONLY BENEFITS ONE'S HEALTH, AND CAN BE used in some home experiments, but it is also useful for a variety of other reasons, which will be discussed in this chapter.

First-Aid Tips

There are several very useful ways to use tea bags for treating minor, yet irritating, conditions.

Sore and Puffy Eyes

If you haven't gotten enough sleep or if you have been crying and find that you have red, puffy eyes, then a couple of used tea bags can come to your rescue and will rejuvenate the appearance of your eyes.

Simply take a couple of used tea bags and soak them in cold water. Squeeze some of the water out and then lie down and lay the tea bags over your closed eyelids. They will mold nicely over them. Leave them there for about five minutes, then take them away and have a look. Your eyes will lose the puffiness.

Any type of tea bag will do, black or green, but green tea is actually more anti-inflammatory than black tea, on account of its beneficial polyphenols. Alternatively, chamomile tea bags work as well.

Just a warning about the tea dribbling over your face onto the pillows! Be aware that tea does stain, so you may want to put an old towel under your head before letting the tea bags do their magic.

Note: If only one eye is affected, and it is red and sore, then this could possibly be an acute eye emergency (acute anterior uveitis or acute glaucoma). If so, seek a medical opinion quickly.

Mouth Ulcers

Tea bags can also soothe and promote healing of painful mouth ulcers.

To treat a mouth ulcer, take a used tea bag and soak it in cold water. Then simply lay it inside the mouth, in contact with the ulcer and leave it for a few minutes. This can be repeated several times a day and will soothe the pain. You may be surprised at how quickly the ulcer begins to heal.

Obviously, if a mouth ulcer persists or increases in size after a week or more, have it checked by your doctor or dentist, as it could be more serious than a simple ulcer.

Scrapes and Small Cuts

Green tea bags have a slight styptic potential. This means that the polyphenols that the green tea contains will help to stop a scrape or cut from oozing blood. Simply cool the used green tea bag in cold water and lay it over the wound or scrape.

It can also help ease the minor burns you can get from touching a hot stove.

Razor Burn

Razor burn can be a very troublesome condition for men and women with sensitive skin. Dabbing the irritated area with a moist green tea bag after shaving can reduce the tendency.

Insect Bites

If you can soothe a flea or insect bite quickly, before the inflammatory response has begun to kick in, then you will limit the amount of irritation. Apply a cold tea bag to the area as soon as possible and leave for about five minutes. After, rub a little toothpaste on it to help with the relief.

Sunburn

If you have not taken adequate precautions with your sunscreen and have actually developed a sunburn, then cold green tea soaks can reduce the pain. Make green tea in the usual way, allow it to go cold, and then soak washclothes in it and lay them over the sunburned area of your skin.

Acne Vulgaris

Acne vulgaris is a skin condition typically affecting teenagers and young adults. It occurs when the skin pores become blocked. The face is mainly affected by acne, but it can also occur on the back, shoulders, and chest. We do not know why it occurs, but it does seem to relate to testosterone—the male hormone. This does not mean that only males get it; women also produce androgenic (male) hormones.

Once a skin pore gets blocked, sebum—skin oil—gets trapped. Bacteria thrive in this and produce an inflammatory effect in the skin. Some will produce the typical acne spots.

While tea will not get rid of acne, drinking green tea may help the body's overall immunity. Green tea washes are worth trying because tea has anti-inflammatory, antiseptic, and antioxidant effects. The simplest way is to use a green tea bag and dab it over the face or affected area when washing. Don't rub it on since rubbing can increase inflammation.

A physician's advice and treatment may well be needed if the acne persists or gets worse.

Deodorant

This may surprise you, but both green and black tea bags are useful deodorants when applied under the arms. Make sure that you then rinse after, since you don't want to risk tea staining on your clothes.

Dandruff and Other Scalp Conditions

Dandruff is a condition that afflicts most people at some point in their lives. For most people, it usually takes care of itself. Unfortunately, some people have an almost continual problem with it and have to shun wearing dark clothes in order to avoid the telltale snowstorm effects on their shoulders. The old medical textbooks call it *pityriasis capitis*. It is undoubtedly the most common condition affecting the scalp.

The skin cells of the scalp are continually renewing themselves. New cells form in the deeper layers of the skin and are gradually pushed upward by the new cells forming beneath. As they reach the surface they become very flat, like tiny plates, and overlap one another. By the time they reach the top the cells are dead and are shed unnoticed.

With dandruff, the skin cell turnover is sped up. In mild cases, tiny flakes of skin are shed to produce a dust-like effect. In more severe cases there is a clumping of skin cells producing embarrassing flakes and snow-storms on dark clothes. Often the scalp feels itchy during the flare up.

People with dandruff often have tiny yeast called *Pityrosporum ovale* on their scalp. Everyone actually has this on their skin, especially on greasy areas such as the scalp, behind the ears, and on the back. The dandruff sufferer, however, is liable to have much more of it. Whether it is the cause or effect is not known, but diminishing the amount often improves the condition.

Using a shampoo with green tea in it may be all that you need. You may also like to try simply using green tea that has cooled as a hair rinse. Use it in this way and then wait a couple of minutes before toweling dry. Often, it will gradually remove the problem after a week or two's use.

Home Uses

Here are some other uses of tea that may never have occurred to you, but which may be of help to you around the home.

Teatime for Your Plants

Tea may be good for plants, since it is antibacterial and full of antioxidants. But it is slightly acidic, so it will only truly help those plants that thrive in acidic soils. Following is a list of plants that may thrive with tea being fed to them:

Fruits that like acid soil:

- Blueberries

Plants that like strong acid soil (pH 5 to 6):

- Azaleas
- Camellias
- Catnip
- Heathers
- Hibiscuses
- Hydrangeas (if you want blue flowers)
- Magnolias
- Rhododendrons
- Tomatoes
- Witch hazel

Plants that like slightly acidic soil or neutral soil (pH 6.5 to 7):

- Anemone

- Alliums
- Begonias
- Roses
- Squashes
- Strawberries (sweeter in acid soil)
- Sunflowers

Plants that like slightly alkaline soils (with a pH of 7 and up), such as figs, irises, lilac, and yucca, will not thank you for watering them with tea!

You may also be interested to know that hydrangeas will grow blue flowers in acidic soil and pink in alkaline. This is not because it is reacting oddly, but because of the effect of pH on the absorption of aluminum from the soil. Acidic soils help its absorption, and in the case of *Hydrangea microphylla* aluminum makes it produce blue flowers. Absence of aluminum turns the flowers pink.

Freshen the Lingerie Drawer

Green tea can be effective in making your underwear drawer smell fresh. You may choose a tea that also has rose or jasmine for added scent. Simply get some loose-leaf tea of this type and place it in a small, thin gossamer or cloth bag. Put one or two of these into your lingerie drawer and be surprised at how it absorbs odors and leaves your clothing smelling fresh.

Smelly Feet

Locker rooms and changing rooms all smell similar—the mustiness of sportswear shoved in lockers and that all pervading stale odor of sweaty feet. Smelly feet are, of course, expected in sports clubs, but for some people, it can be an embarrassing problem that impinges upon daily life.

Each person has about three to four million sweat glands over the body, a large proportion of them being on the hands and feet. Sweat itself hardly smells. The pungent odor of smelly feet comes from fatty acids being produced by bacterial action on the perspired fluid.

If you are afflicted with smelly feet, then having a regular green tea footbath for twenty minutes at a time will help.

Footwear is often a large part of the problem. Plastic and synthetic linings in sneakers and shoes prevent perspiration from evaporating and, because shoes do not absorb the perspiration, they have the effect of keeping the foot moist. This permits greater bacterial action through more fatty acid production. Nylon socks and tights have the same effect as synthetic shoe lining. Cotton has a limited absorption capacity before it gets moist and slightly soggy. Wool also becomes soggy quickly. Ideally, one should use socks made of 60 to 70 percent wool with 40 to 30 percent man-made fibers.

Socks, shoes, and sneakers should be worn for only one day at a time. Sneaker, particularly are ideal for creating sweaty and smelly feet. Here again a green tea bag placed into the toe of each shoe every night will tend to absorb the smell. Use fresh bags each time. They will also work best if they have been slightly moistened, but not be wet when they are placed in the shoes.

Grime Remover

Mirrors are often tricky to get clean, but used moist black tea bags are excellent for getting rid of stains, toothpaste, and face powder from the mirror's surface. They are also good at getting rid of grime on floors and linoleum. Your kitchen countertops may also benefit from a rubdown with them. Obviously, though, just make sure that you wipe thoroughly afterwards, or you may leave unwanted tea stains.

Chapter Seventeen

Tea in Literature

Bring me a cup of tea and The Times.

Queen Victoria (1819–1901),
upon her ascension to the throne in 1837

IT IS NOT SURPRISING THAT TEA, WHICH IS ENJOYED BY
people all over the globe, should be used in one form or another as an
ingredient of or a backdrop for various fictional works. It is such a natural
thing to have people pouring tea, sipping tea, peering suspiciously over
the rim of their teacup, or adding a few drops of poison to the oolong in
the Queen Ann teapot.

At the start of this book, I stated that I was deeply influenced by the
Judge Dee novels by Robert Van Gulik. Judge Dee drinks tea in the same
way that Sherlock Holmes puffs meditatively on his pipe. Sipping a pot of
tea is the same as a "three-pipe problem" for Holmes. By the time Dee has
drunk and cogitated on the clues, all becomes clear to him.

In one of the short Judge Dee stories, two of his assistants, Ma Joong
and Chiao Tai, are drinking wine in a tavern while on a break in an investigation. They are discussing the case, but find that the wine is not helping
them, since it is only good when one is carefree. They find it impossible
to concentrate on their drinking, which is important to them, when they
have a problem to solve. Chiao Tai concludes that is the reason why Judge
Dee is always sipping tea.

So let us have a look at how other writers use tea in their books.

Charles Dickens (1812–1870)

Charles Dickens is one writer responsible for giving us a picture of the many faces of London in the nineteenth century. No one described the social squalor, the inequalities, and the rampant corruption of the city at that time better than he. Dickens had lived in abject poverty, and at the tender age of ten, he had seen his father thrown into debtor's prison, leaving him to the devices of the Warren's Blacking Company, where he worked in a rat-infested factory sticking labels on jars of shoe polish for ten hours a day. The experience made him determined to escape poverty and make something of himself. Later in life, he became the richest author of his day, feted across continents and declared a national treasure.

His works are peppered with people drinking tea, visiting tearooms, and plotting over tea. In his great novel of 1838, *Oliver Twist*, he has the orphaned Oliver go with his gruel bowl in hand to the portly, cock-hatted beadle of the workhouse, Mr. Bumble, and utter the immortal words, "Please, sir, I want some more."[45]

Things go from bad to worse, and Oliver is involved in many adventures, escaping from the workhouse and falling in with the Artful Dodger and Fagin, the master of a gang of boy pickpockets and thieves.

Meanwhile, Mr. Bumble is courting a lady, Mrs. Corney, the matron of the workhouse where Oliver was born. He has come out of the snow to see her and the prospect of a cup of tea from her very small, black teapot most appealing. She invites him to join her for tea, and Dickens describes the scene in comic detail:

"Sweet? Mr. Bumble," inquired the matron, taking up the sugar-basin.

"Very sweet, indeed, ma'am," replied Mr. Bumble. He fixed his eyes on Mrs. Corney as he said this: and if ever a beadle looked tender, Mr. Bumble was that beadle at the moment.

The beadle drank his tea to the last drop, finished a piece of toast, whisked the crumbs off his knees, wiped his lips, and deliberately kissed the matron.

Further, Dickens empathized with orphans, waifs, and the poor. He had managed to elevate his station in life, and so he allowed Pip Gargery to be elevated by an unknown benefactor in his novel, *Great Expectations.*

In the book, Miss Havisham, whom Pip believes to be his benefactor, was jilted on her wedding day and lives in a crumbling mansion, dressed always in her wedding gown, determined to have her ward, Estella, break men's hearts. And the main heart to be broken is Pip's. Once in London, though, Pip becomes a tea snob:

> I rang for the tea, and the waiter, reappearing with his magic clue, brought in by degrees some fifty adjuncts to that refreshment but of tea not a glimpse. A teaboard, cups and saucers, plates, knives and forks (including carvers), spoons (various), saltcellars, a meek little muffin confined with the utmost precaution under a strong iron cover, Moses in the bullrushes typified by a soft bit of butter in a quantity of parsley, a pale loaf with a powdered head, two proof impressions of the bars of the kitchen fire-place on triangular bits of bread, and ultimately a fat family urn: which the waiter staggered in with, expressing in his countenance burden and suffering. After a prolonged absence at this stage of the entertainment, he at length came back with a casket of precious appearance containing twigs. These I steeped in hot water, and so from the whole of these appliances extracted one cup of I don't know what, for Estella.[46]

Baroness Orzy (1865–1947)

Baroness Orzy's most famous character was the Scarlet Pimpernel, the alter ego of Sir Percy Blakeney, an aristocratic fop during the Reign of Terror that followed the start of the French Revolution. In 1905, the same year that Orzy made his debut, a character who is less well known today also created quite a stir. This was the Old Man in the Corner, who in a series of short stories solves sensational crimes with pure logic while sitting in an A.B.C tea shop in London. He amuses himself by tying complicated knots in a piece of string as he explains all to Polly Burton, a journalist. The stories are all set at the turn of the twentieth century.

C. P. Snow (1905–1980)

Charles Percy Snow, later to become Lord Snow, was a scientist, novelist, and British civil servant. His first foray into literature was a whodunit entitled *Death Under Sail*, a delightful 1932 sailing novel set in the Norfolk Broads of England.

Roger Mills is a Harley Street doctor taking a sailing holiday when he is found dead at the tiller by his six guests, shot through the heart. Yet Mills has an enigmatic smile on his face. Two detectives enter the scene, Finbow—an amateur detective—and the official, Detective-Sergeant Aloysius Birrel. Finbow is, of course, the main man who solves the case. Tea is Finbow's delight. He actually goes everywhere with a little container in his pocket in which he keeps "the finest tea in the world."

Agatha Christie (1890–1976)

Agatha Christie is known throughout the world as the "Queen of Crime." She was born Agatha Clarissa Miller and was educated at her home in Torquay. Her father, Frederick Miller, was an American with an independent income who died when Agatha was eleven. In 1912, she met Archie Christie, a young aviator who had applied to join the fledgling Royal Flying Corps. When the Great War started in 1914, they married, then Colonel Christie went off to fly in war-torn France while Agatha became a nurse in the Voluntary Aid Detachment (VAD) of the Red Cross Hospital in Torquay before becoming a qualified dispenser. It was there that she started to learn about poisons and where she stared to write her first detective novel, *The Mysterious Affair at Styles*. It was several years before it was published, but it was the start of a stellar career that would see her write eighty novels and short story collections, nineteen plays, and six novels under the name of Mary Westmacott.

Poisoning was by far her favored method of murder, and all sorts of people were dispatched through poison being added to all manner of tea accouterments.

It would be unethical, not to say mean-spirited and party-pooping, to reveal the plots of any of her wonderful novels, but in the following poisons are to be found in these novels:

> *The Mirror Cracked from Side to Side*—cyanide
> *And Then There Were None*—cyanide
> *A Pocketful of Rye*—cyanide
> *4.50 from Paddington*—arsenic
> *The Pale Horse*—thallium
> *A Pocketful of Rye*—taxine
> *Crooked House*—physostigmine
> *Sad Cypress*—morphine
> *Curtain*—morphine and physostigmine

Every single one of them makes an ideal accompaniment to tea—the novels, that is!

Chapter Eighteen

Tasseography: Teacup Fortune-telling

Going to the fortune teller's was just as good as going to the opera, and the cost scarcely a trifle more—ergo, I will disguise myself and go again, one of these days, when other amusements fail.

Mark Twain (1835–1910),
in a letter to Orion Clemens, February 6, 1861

I HAVE ALWAYS LOVED TEA. IN FACT, WHEN I WAS A YOUNG lad in Scotland, I spent a holiday in the highlands with an aunt and uncle. My uncle used to laugh at how much tea I would drink and told me that I was "a real tea jenny, just like your aunt."

It was only later that I realized that she actually was a "tea jenny," or a tea witch. "Jenny" was a generic term for witch in the seventeenth century, and it persisted ever after. A tea jenny was the name given to someone who could read tea leaves. And that is just what my aunt showed me, declaring "it is only a bit of fun."

I wasn't so sure back then. And I am still not, because she seemed to be very accurate in what she told me.

For now, though, I say to you, gentle reader: it's just for a bit of fun.

Ancient Divination

People have always wanted to be able to see into the future. The reasons why seem to be as diverse as are the different types of tea. Some people have a desire to know whether they will become rich, live long, find love and happiness, or have the satisfaction that they will get even with someone who has done them wrong.

In the long distant past, people who could read signs were much sought after and could achieve a position of some standing in society. There is evidence that forms of divination were practiced in China, Egypt, Chaldea, and Babylonia as long ago as 4000 BC.

During the Shang dynasty (1776–1122 BC), "oracles bones" were used to answer all sorts of questions, ranging from the weather to suitable suitors for the nobility. The bones tended to be scapulae or shoulder blades of oxen, but sometimes, the plates of turtle shells were also used. A question would be inscribed or written on the oracle bone, which would then be heated until it cracked. The pattern of cracking and fissuring would then be interpreted.

Sometime around 1000 BC, the famed *Classic Book of Changes*, or *I Ching*, as it is commonly known as, was written. It is said to be the oldest book on divination in the world and may have been invented as a system much earlier than that. Indeed, according to legend it is said to date to the third millennium BC. It is a hexagram system in which sixty-four sets of hexagrams (figures made up of six lines) represent oracular pronouncements. A question is asked, and some yarrow stalks or three coins are cast to reveal which hexagrams will yield the answer.

At around the same time, the ancient Egyptians were practicing divination through astrology and also through the interpretation of dreams. The *Chester Beatty* Papyri date to the twelfth dynasty (1991–1786 BC) and give a record of such dream interpretations.

In ancient Babylon, priests practiced the art of *hepatoscopy*, or examination of the liver from a slaughtered animal, usually a sheep. By doing so the Babylonians thought that they could see the will of the gods. They chose the liver because it was believed to be the source of blood, the precious fluid that gave a creature life. The lobulated organ was thought to be of huge significance, with each lobe representing a deity. Several bronze models of the liver have come down to us from antiquity, with the lobes inscribed with cuneiform writing indicating the meaning of anomalies that might be found.

Hepatoscopy was just one type of *extispicy*—the practice of examining animal and bird entrails to divine the purpose of the gods. It was practiced by other cultures, including the Romans and the Etruscans. Indeed, in ancient Rome, there was a College of Augurs where men could be trained in the reading of entrails, cloud formations, and the movement of birds and hens in order to read the future. Emperor Claudius had actually been trained as an augur. Indeed, it may have been thanks to his intuitive skills and imagination that he was able to survive the rule of his infamous nephew Caligula, who believed that his uncle had the gift of speaking to the gods on his behalf.

In ancient Greece, oracles were consulted to determine propitious days to go to war, to make peace, or to seek general guidance. It was believed that the gods also gave messages to people as they slept, thus sleep temples were used in the treatment of patients, it being thought that divine knowledge and the meaning of illness could come from a dream experienced in the temple.

However, once the major religions of the world were established, all of the old gods were swept away. Divination was no longer considered divine but was relegated to mere fortune-telling or even witchcraft.

The Dangerous Art of Fortune-telling

Britain was a particularly dangerous place to try and earn money by reading the fortune of one's comrades, no matter how much people wanted to know what the future held for them. It was gradually driven underground so that fortune-tellers took to the roads, visiting fairs and towns, just staying long enough to have their palms crossed with silver enough times to buy provisions and then fleeing before someone accused them of practicing witchcraft or necromancy.

In Britain, a witchcraft act was passed in 1563, during Queen Elizabeth I's reign. It made witchcraft illegal and punishable by death. And fortune-telling was considered witchcraft. Between 1645 and 1647,

Matthew Hopkins, the witch-finder general of England, was instrumental in ordering two hundred women put to death.

In Europe during the sixteenth century, hundreds of thousands of men and women found themselves denounced as witches. They were subjected to a host of torture instruments, including the rack, the iron maiden, the Scavenger's Daughter, thumbscrews, pincers, burning stools, ducking stools, and more. In Spain, the grand inquisitor Torquemada condemned ninety-seven thousand people and sent over ten thousand luckless individuals to the stake as witches.

Things were certainly not easier in America during the seventeenth century, as events in Salem, Massachusetts, were to prove in 1692, when the infamous Salem Witchcraft Trials took place. Seemingly it all started when Tituba, a slave owned by the Reverend Samuel Parris, started to recount tales of her native Barbados to Betty, the reverend's daughter, Betty's cousin Abigail, and several of their friends. She described the beaches and the sugarcane that grew in profusion and told them tales about the witchdoctors, who could cast spells, heal the sick, and foretell the future. So enthralled by these tales were the two girls that they pestered Tituba to show them how to tell the future. And so she did, by dripping egg whites from a freshly hatched white chicken egg into a bowl of water. It had to be done carefully so that the egg white would remain suspended in the water, allowing her to use it for *scrying*, as a crystal ball is used. Thus began a little group of young girls who would meet clandestinely with Tituba and who would experiment with fortune-telling.

Unfortunately, Betty soon began to have fits, which may have been hysterical attacks brought on by her guilty feelings about the meetings and the things that the girls were dabbling in. Tituba was persuaded to try to help her by baking a witch cake made of rye and some of Betty's urine. This was baked and fed to a dog in the belief that it could transfer the ailment from Betty to the dog. The Reverend Parris found out about it and was furious. He beat a confession out of Tituba and declared her a witch.

Tituba was the first "witch" to confess in Salem. But not only did she confess about her own crimes, but she also said that there was an active coven in Salem and named two women, Sarah Osborne and Sarah Goode, as fellow witches. Tituba was jailed, but between June and September of 1692, nineteen men and women were convicted of witchcraft and taken to Gallows Hill, where they were hanged.

Back in Britain, things started to improve for the fortune-telling fraternity. King George II repealed the statute in 1735, and introduced a new witchcraft act. This permitted fortune-tellers to live, albeit that they could expect to be tossed in prison for a year and probably then spend a good amount of time in the public pillory having fruit, bad eggs, and dung thrown at them. It is a wonder that anyone dared gaze into the crystal ball, read tarot cards, or keep the fortune-telling art going.

And then along came a new drink with fortune-telling potential: tea.

Tasseography

It is not clear who first started reading tea leaves to try to predict the future. It may have been someone in China. Certainly the Chinese did use oracles as mentioned above, as well as a form of fortune-telling that involves pouring molten metals into water to produce a solid pattern. The method involved determining the meaning of the shape that was produced.

As tea spread around the world, so, too, did the art of tasseography. The word comes from the French *tasse*, (cup), which itself comes from the Arabic *tassa*; and the Greek *graphos*, meaning reading or writing. Hence "tea-reading."

Wherever tea found its way, so did tea-readers. It is still practiced in the Middle East and wherever tea is imbibed. The method also includes the reading of coffee grounds.

The Victorian era seems to have been the age when tasseography was developed into an art form. Although it has the reputation of being practiced by Gypsy fortune-tellers, with the ubiquitous consumption of tea in the nineteenth century it seemed to have developed into a rather respectable and amusing afternoon tea party pastime. People from all walks of life practiced it and used it as a sort of party game when the conversation was getting dull and the cucumber sandwiches had run out.

Carl Jung and the Universal Unconscious

Carl Jung (1875–1961) continues to be one of the most famous names in psychology. He was an associate of Sigmund Freud for many years until he broke away and founded his own discipline of analytical psychology. He was deeply interested in symbolism and the practices of fortune-tellers, astrologers, and occult practitioners.

Jung believed that man had a consciousness, and that beneath it, there was a personal unconscious (although it was not based on sexuality or motivated by sex, as Freud believed), but his concept went even deeper. He believed that beyond the personal unconscious, there is a shared collective unconscious. This he believed was not just inherited from one's forebears, but was in fact shared by all members of the human race, and was literally a universal unconscious. It is here that he believed that the meanings of symbols are to be found. Essentially, since symbols have a deep meaning, if one can see a pattern, one can interpret it against the universal unconscious.

So with tasseography, or any other type of interpretive fortune-telling, the theory is that the reader uses his intuitive faculties to tune into the universal conscious, which is the same unconscious that is shared with the person who is seeking the reading, and the symbols that the universe is throwing out will be given relevance.

Just a Bit of Fun

The art of tasseography and the universal unconscious may be hard to swallow. But the point about tasseography is that it has been practiced by many people for hundreds of years, and if viewed in a light-hearted manner and not taken too seriously, it can provide quite an entertaining diversion at the end of a cup of tea.

Next, we'll discuss how to actually read tea leaves. But first, here are a few things not to do:

- Do not think that you are an oracle
- Do not predict death or illness

- Do not read your own leaves for anything other than fun
- Do not take it too seriously

Choose Your Cup and Saucer

The cup that you use for reading tea leaves should be pleasing to the eye and practical for tasseography. Only you can decide what is pleasing to you, but for ease of reading, a relatively wide brim and fairly shallow cup is best. It is best to use one with a handle, rather than a handle-less cup, and you will need a saucer, as it is involved in the reading.

It is generally practical to use a cup that is white inside and devoid of patterns, although you can find cups that are specially made for tasseography. Some are even collectible. If you want, you can seek out antique cups from the nineteenth century. They generally have the cups divided into segments to make the process of reading quite simple. Some are divided into twelve sections; others into fifty-two, like the number of cards in a deck. Some have symbols printed on them to make your search for symbols easier. In this case, the individual symbols inscribed on the cup have a significance—for example, an arrow generally means news—but a tea leaf symbol landing on it would indicate news relating to that symbol suggested by the leaves. Thus, if a money sign were found on it, it would indicate that there would soon be news of money. Other cups have playing card suits and numbers so that the adept reader can combine cartomancy with tasseography, and others have numbers so that numerology and tasseography can be used in tandem. The appearance of a symbol similar to a card suit or to a number can take on the significance of a suit or of the number.

The follow are a list of the significance of suits:

- Hearts—emotions (love affairs, friendships, and relationships)
- Clubs—words, negotiations, matters of commerce, and business
- Diamonds—the material realm, property, and social status
- Spades—problems, arguments, negativity, and loss

The following are a list of the significance of numbers:

- 1—new beginnings, renewal
- 2—kindness, generosity
- 3—intuition, magic, advantage
- 4—stability, calm, the home
- 5—travel, adventure, things in motion
- 6—love, truth
- 7—magic, luck
- 8—business, wealth, success
- 9—satisfaction, completion, accomplishment

You should already be beginning to see how these symbols in a teacup could be useful. Indeed, imagine the cup being divided into four zones, which correlates with the four suits, so symbols landing in those sectors will have their set significance. Or you can divide the cup into nine sectors. The essence of reading tea leaves is to have a system, but you can certainly create your own system. As long as you stick to the method that you choose before the reading, you should be able to do an honest reading.

Choose Your Tea

You can use any type of tea leaves for tasseography, but consider that the smaller the leaves, the more they can aggregate into patterns. Long-leafed tea may make more robust patterns, but there will probably be less symbols formed. Matcha, powdered tea, can be used, because it forms a suspension, but just make sure that the person who is having the reading has drunk enough of it so that it can be swirled well enough to leave patterns. Alternatively, you can use tea bags, which contain fannings and are actually very good for tasseography. Just snip the bag open and brew the tea in a teapot.

Enjoy the Cup of Tea As You Chat

Drinking the tea and chatting with the person whose cup is to be read is part of the whole experience. The two people get to know one another and feel more at ease. First, a pot of tea is brewed, and when it is ready two cups are poured, one for the reader and one for the querent, the person who is having the reading. Note that no strainer is to be used, since you need the leaves to form the symbols!

Talk while you drink should be quite informal and superficial since the aim is to do the reading as it comes rather than to pick up clues about the person and then to make the reading fit what you think he or she wants to hear. That is called "cold reading," and it has to be admitted that it is a skill that people can develop in order to give the person the message that he or she wants to receive. It is sham reading, which is more akin to conjuring and mentalism instead of tasseography.

So feel free to chat away about all sorts of topics as you both drink the tea. The reader should tell the querent when he or she gets down to the dregs to swirl the cup around and around counterclockwise three times with his or her left hand (or the right hand if the person is left-handed), then upend the cup to drain any fluid away into the saucer. As they do the swirling ask the person to focus on what it is that he or she wants to know. Once the reader has upended the cup, he or she should hold it there for a count of ten.

You are almost ready to do the reading. But first, you need to know what method to use and have some knowledge of the symbols that may show up.

Choose Your Method of Reading

There are several ways that the reading can be done. Below are a few suggestions.

The Spiral

If using this method, the reader begins by holding the cup with the handle pointing at the person having the reading done. The symbols are then read in a spiral manner, going around clockwise in an imaginary spiral through the three areas of the cup. The top third of the cup represents the present and the near future (up to three months) and the influences that are surrounding the querent at this time of her life. The middle part of the cup is the future over the next few months to a year, and the bottom third is the far future. The very bottom of the cup represents the things that are not even on the querent's horizon. They may be totally unexpected. Some readers feel that leaves left on the bottom of the cup generally have a negative import and represent bad luck. You determine how you will personally interpret that and stick with it.

The Two Hemispheres

Some readers use the handle to relate to the querent and to matters close to home. All symbols on this half of the cup, with the handle in the center, relate to the individual and things that will directly affect him or her. Symbols that point at the handle relate to things that are going to have an influence upon the querent, whereas symbols pointing away are things or influences that are moving away. A symbol for money could indicate money coming or money being lost, depending on its relationship to the handle.

Symbols on the opposite side of the cup are not personal or related to the home. They may relate to the actions or attitudes of others. If they are pointing toward the querent, then they may have an effect, but if away they may relate to something that the other person is going to take away.

This method may be more adapted to the sort of yes or no questions, where someone wants to know what they should do. It is not up to the reader, of course, to give a definitive answer but to do the reading according to what the symbols and their positions say. Once again, the depth may tell you whether the influencing symbols are related to the present or near future, some months hence, or the far future.

The Horoscope Method

This is actually a method ideally suited for the types of "fortune-telling cups" that you can find on the market. A horoscope pattern is inscribed on the cup, dividing it into twelve segments. Yet, there is a simpler method that you can use, which simply requires your own two hands.

Place a cup in front of you with the handle pointing away from you. Now hold it in both hands so that your index fingers touch the handle and your thumbs touch the back of the cup, opposite the handle. Look into the cup and imagine lines running from the handle into the middle of the cup and lines joining the skin creases of the index fingers also running to the center of the cup. Notice that there will be three sectors formed from the left index finger and three from the right finger. Each sector will be about thirty degrees, and the three on each side make a right angle. Looked at as a whole, you will have six imaginary segments.

If you overlap your thumbs so that the two skin creases correspond, you can also see three other sectors formed on each side. If you prefer, you can simply reverse the cup and touch your index fingers together on the side opposite the handle. The whole point is to do it so that you can imagine the cup being divided into twelve sectors.

Now place the cup so that the handle is pointing to the left. Imagine the twelve sectors on the cup. This represents the horoscope chart. Each sector represents a "house"—in astrological terms, a sphere of one's life. They are arranged so that the ascendant—the appearance of the stars at the moment of birth, or the point that a question is posed—is on the left. This is entirely appropriate in teacup reading, since the question is posed at the time of the reading. The houses are arranged counterclockwise from the handle (ascendant), so house one is immediately below the handle and house twelve is immediately above it.

The use of your hands merely provides a convenient way of reading the teacup. It does not have to be an entirely accurate division into twelve houses, but it should be consistent. It is important that you, as the reader, know how the cup is divided up and that you have a natural way of doing the division no matter what cup you use since you simply use your own anatomical landmarks.

The follow are descriptions of the twelve houses:

1. The self—this has to do with the querent. It relates to their physical self and their health.

2. Value and money—this is fortune, self-esteem, self-worth, and all things to do with possessions and finance.

3. Communication, travel, and siblings—this has to do with communication of things, ideas, and thoughts. It is also connected with siblings and neighbors.

4. The home, family, and property—this has to do with the mother.

5. Recreation, leisure, and pleasure—this is love and sex, gambling, and children.

6. Health and employment—this is the individual's health, work, and all matters pertaining to him or her. This also covers pets and animals.

7. Partnerships—this is mainly about relationships. These can be personal and/or business related.

8. The house of rebirth, regeneration, and new beginnings—this has to do with birth, death, surgery, healing, wills, inheritance, and gifts. Think of new beginnings.

9. Travel—this can be extended beyond long journeys to mean far off places, things connected with far off places, or strangers entering and having an influence upon a person. It can also relate to law and legal situations.

10. Career and position—this has to do with ambitions, aspirations, attainment, success, responsibility, occupation, and preoccupation.

11. Hopes, wishes, and dreams—this is about friends, groups, organizations, clubs, and societies.

12. The hidden house—this deals with secrets, the occult, and psychic matters. It can also be hospitals, situations, and the subconscious mind.

The depth of the leaves follows the same pattern as with the spiral—nearer the rim represents the present and the near future; the middle third represents the next six months to a year; and the lower third to the bottom represent the years ahead in the far future.

The Meaning of the Signs

The following interpretations are fairly common and have been used for centuries. They are not meant to be didactic but to give the reader enough knowledge to allow his or her intuition to take over and to weave the narrative that unfolds. The horoscope method and the spiral seem to offer the best chance of giving the querent a narrative ranging from the present to the future. The two hemispheres method is more suited to a specific question that the querent wants to know an answer to (for example, should I take a job, should I follow a particular course, or should I avoid it?).

Imagination is needed when reading the signs, since the patterns may not show an actual shape, but two or three leaves clumped near each other may suggest a pattern to you, rather in the same way that constellations suggest patterns in the sky.

Please note that there is no reason why the reader cannot alter or add to the meaning of any sign if she feels that it means something else to her. This is the nature of any of the so-called interpretive arts; the signs are there to strike a chord in the individual's mind, to stimulate his or her own intuition. So, simply use the following interpretations as guides to stimulate your unconscious mind.

A FEW GENERALITIES

Long lines are regarded as roads and usually indicate a change in fortune. If they are surrounded by lots of dots, then money is to be gained. Or the road may be a health line, and good health or a good outcome is likely.

Wavy lines indicate agitation or imply that the way will not be smooth.

Dots from individual leaves or fannings generally mean money will be gained.

Circles indicate that there is fortune or that matters are complete.

Acorn

This is a good omen. It is generally indicative of happiness and fulfillment. It also means that things that are going to thrive—"mighty oaks from little acorns grow." So it could mean a new venture that will reap success. The nearer to the brim the arcorn is, the more imminent the reward. The farther away, it will be a more long-term project.

Aircraft

This sign indicates elevation or flying, so projects should take off. If it seems to be near clouds, then those could indicate some obstacles or stormy weather that impedes the success, but the hopes of a successful venture are there. An aircraft near any other "obstacle" sign usually indicates that the obstacle will be overcome.

Alligator or Crocodile

This is a warning sign. It means that things are not what they seem. There may be treachery afoot, and you need to be wary of people who may let you down. This may be unexpected, so you need to keep your wits about you, just as you would if there was a real alligator or crocodile in the vicinity.

Anchor

This is generally a successful sign, implying stability and constancy. If near the brim, it means that love and affection will last. Deeper down is an indication of successful undertaking by water or over water. Like an anchor that holds on, so there will not be loss in this venture, whether it is romantic or fiscal.

Angel

There is a protective influence over you at the moment.

Animals

The reading depends on the type of animal and how well formed it is. The clearer it is, the greater the influence; the fainter, the hazier the effect, but it will be there. The following are common animals and their appropriate readings:

- Ass—patience is needed
- Bat—take care—there may be trouble ahead
- Bear—potential danger
- Cat—treachery or deception, although some readers take it as a sign of good luck
- Cow—good luck and prosperity, especially if pointing at the handle
- Dog—a faithful friend will help you out; also unconditional love
- Elephant—there is something to be remembered
- Fox—there could be craft and deceit at work
- Goat—enemies may be ready to butt you
- Horse—a lover may influence you
- Lamb—pleasure will be found in this activity
- Lion—there is a powerful friend who will help and protect you
- Mouse—you may be the victim of theft or burglary, so take care
- Pig—there could be good luck, in that treasure may be found in unlikely places; or this could be a warning against greed
- Wolf—there could be secrets that you don't know about, and someone could be going about matters in a secretive way
- Zebra—adventure in a far off place is indicated

ANT OR ANTS

This indicates that there will be lots of activity and lots of constructive effort and general business. If related to business or money, it will be successful.

ARCH OR DOOR

There is an opening or an opportunity ahead.

ARROW

This sign means some sort of communication is on its way. It will generally be soon. In most readers' view, the direction of the arrow indicates the type of news. If it is pointing upwards toward the rim, it is good news. If it points down, the news is bad or unfavorable. The horoscope method gives a good indication of which sphere of life will be affected, as well as which sphere the news comes from.

AXE

This indicates that you will hack your way out of a problem.

BABY

This may indicate a new arrival. This could actually be a new life, or it could be a symbolic new start.

BAG

If the bag is like a sack, then someone may have set a trap for you. Or, someone may have stolen or is preparing to steal from you. If it is shaped like a handbag, then it may have the opposite meaning, and someone has good things in store for you.

BALLOON

Fun and excitement are looming.

BASKET

A basket is generally a sign of bounty and good things—possibly a purchase or a gift.

BED

You need to get your rest before acting. Sleep on it before you act. Can also mean an illness.

BEES

Rather like ants, bees indicate prosperity, activity, and success.

BELL

This stands for recognition and celebration. Two bells could be marriage.

BICYCLE

You are on your own in this activity, but you should be pleased about it. You are working under your own steam.

BIRD OR BIRDS

Generally, a bird means good luck. The more there are, the better the luck. The following birds have these meanings:

- Chicken—this may be quite distinct. It implies fertility and the successful completion of a task. Chickens have always been regarded as potent symbols of fortune, which is why they were used by augurs (professional soothsayers) in ancient Rome
- Duck—success and trade; generally calmness
- Eagle—success and triumph
- Owl—trouble or agitation. An owl is not a good omen
- Parrot—bad news. There is a plot in motion
- Peacock—luxury
- Raven—bad news is coming
- Swan—good luck. A lover may be nearby
- Vulture—ominous omen. There could be trouble and agitation ahead, and someone waiting to pick over the bones of the fallen

BOAT

This indicates a discovery of some sort.

BOOK

Study or research is needed. If it is open, then a revelation lies ahead.

BOOT

Travel may lie ahead. If it is an old-fashioned boot, then you may need to get rid of something old.

Bottle

Celebration is ahead.

Butterfly

This is a sign of pleasure, of indulgence, and of appreciation of nature. Or, it may be a frivolous pleasure.

Cabbage

This is a sign of jealousy. It may mean that you will be jealous, or you will be the object of jealousy. Just remember that jealousy is a useless emotion that does nothing positive. It can eat into you, so work to get rid of it.

Cage

This indicates that a proposal is nearby. But watch out, as it could be a situation in which you will be trapped or find it hard to extricate yourself from in the future.

Castle

Strength and protection are available. You may need to defend yourself.

Chain

There is strength in this undertaking. If the chain is broken, the undertaking may break down.

Child

This implies the innocence of childhood. It can be interpreted that you need to go into a situation with the open eyes of an adult and not be too gullible, like a child. It can also indicate that you will incur an expense.

Clock

This is a sign of illness. Note that this does not necessarily relate to the person; it can possibly relate to someone close to the person.

CLOUDS

Obstacles are ahead, possibly gloomy; possibly a storm is ahead.

CLOWN

Happiness, humor, and frivolity are in store.

COFFIN

This indicates an ending, such as the end of a situation, the end of a business, or the end of a period of stress.

COMET

The unexpected is coming. It can be a sudden unexpected happening related to whatever sphere it is found in.

CRADLE

This means that things are going to increase after a recent beginning.

CROSS

This is a sign of suffering, as Jesus suffered on the cross. There will be a period of anguish or difficulty, but there will be regeneration following it. It is therefore a sign of difficulty followed by hope. It implies that one needs faith, although not necessarily religious faith. A cross within a circle indicates that there will be detainment, hospitalization, or some sort of enforced inactivity.

CROWN

A regal sign, so there will be success and honor ahead.

DAGGER

There is danger lurking.

DICE

There will be luck involved. But the luck will probably be with you.

Dragon

Great riches are to come. This can be financial, spiritual, or intellectual, depending on where it is found in the cup.

Drum

This is a warning. Beat the drum to warn others.

Ear

You will hear something to your advantage.

Egg

A very lucky sign. The more of them, the better.

Eye

Look at a situation in detail. There may be trouble. The symbol of the "evil eye" is an ancient one, going all the way to ancient Egypt.

Face

There is a discovery to be made.

Fairy

A romantic sign; generally a happy symbol.

Fan

This sign has to do with flirtation.

Feather

You need to concentrate.

Fence

There is a barrier around you, but it is not insurmountable. You can get over it.

FLIES

Irritation is at hand.

FLOCKS

This can be sheep, birds, and so forth. It is just an impression that you may get from the appearance of lots of small leaves. It indicates crowds, gatherings, and meetings.

FLOWERS

These are generally good signs. Flowers are given as tokens of appreciation, so they can indicate gifts, love, or respect. While you may not be able to identify a precise pattern, it is what the pattern suggests to the reader:

- Clover—good luck is with you
- Daffodil—wealth and new prospects will spring up, since it is a spring flower
- Daisy—simple pleasures abound; also, prospects will spring up
- Fern—there may be changes about to take place
- Ivy—loyal friends may do you service
- Lily—this is virtue and truth; honesty will be the best policy
- Roses—love, commitment, success
- Violet—modesty is the best policy; not a time to be bigheaded or hedonistic

FRUIT

These are fortunate signs of bountifulness and fruitfulness in relation to the sphere in which it is found. The following have various readings:

- Apple—this means that there is bountifulness, health, and creativity. It is also enlightenment, as in the apple that Eve gave to Adam, so it could indicate a Eureka moment in whatever sphere of life it is indicated

- Banana—also a sign of plenty. It can also be a sign to be cautious, as in the way that one can slip on a banana peel
- Grapes—success in love
- Orange—sweet success is coming
- Lemon—there will be success but not in the main undertaking; rather in some secondary matter. One does not eat a lemon on its own, but it is great as a garnish or additive
- Pear—similar to apples
- Pineapple—there may be some illicit activity

GUN

There is danger. Be wary.

HARP

A good time of harmony and peace, and possibly of love, is on its way.

HAT

A sign of honor.

HEART

As you may expect, this is a sign of love and affection.

HORN

This may be a cornucopia—a horn of plenty. Or it could be a sign of valor if it is a hunting horn. There may be something that needs to be proclaimed or announced to the world.

HOURGLASS

There may be danger, and time may be running out in some endeavor.

HOUSE

Home is safety, and this is a sign of security and success.

JAR

This is a sign of provision. You can use your stored-up assets to see you through.

JUG

There is enough of what you need at the moment, but it will not last, much in the way that a jug is only used temporarily.

KETTLE

This can be a sign of power (steam) or a sign that something is brewing up (a quarrel).

KEY

The key unlocks the door to opportunity. Use whatever is involved wisely, and you will unlock the success that you need.

KITE

Just as a kite soars into the sky, so can you achieve great heights. This is a good sign.

KNIFE

This is a sign of caution, just as is the dagger. If you see crossed knives, then there will be bad news.

LADDER

There is opportunity to climb and advance.

LADY

There may be help from a female.

LAMP

There will be illumination and enlightenment in the sphere this sign is associated with.

LEAVES

Success and happiness are coming.

LETTER

News is on its way. The nature of that news, whether good or bad, is indicated by the sphere of life it is associated with. It may be important documentation or information that you have been waiting for.

LOCK

There is an obstacle ahead, and you will have to find the key.

MAN

Expect a visitor.

MASK

Be wary of people in an undertaking. They may be playing a role and may not be trustworthy. Alternatively, this can indicate a party.

MERMAID

This traditional symbol is one of enchantment and temptation. You may need to use all your resources and willpower to resist, but that may be the sensible option since there can be no life with something as exotic as this. It may be glamorous, but it is not of the real world. Be careful and don't be swayed.

MOON

Just as the moon has its different phases, the moon in the teacup has different meanings:

- New moon—romance and new beginnings
- Full moon—success and happiness

- Waning moon—things are on their way out. This is not a time to start something new. Wait and be prudent.

Mountains

A journey is ahead, although it may not be a physical journey. It may be long and hazardous, but the effort may well be worth it.

Mushrooms

There may be a change of home.

Nails

There may be pain and anguish.

Necklace

You'll have success and conquest. A win is indicated.

Oak Tree

Good health and strength are near.

Racquet

It is a time for fun and games.

Saw

You will have to work hard and skillfully.

Scales

There may be something related to justice and the law.

Scissors

Expect disagreement and a quarrel.

Snake

Treachery and duplicity abound. Be wary.

Spider

There may be someone spinning a web of deceit. You may need to be diplomatic.

Star

A good sign of hope and great prospects.

Spoon

Good luck.

Sun

Great fortune is shining on you.

Teapot

There will be a meeting and a discussion.

Tortoise

Things are going to move slowly, but they will happen eventually.

Trees

It is a sign that things are going to happen naturally. A good sign of fruitfulness.

Triangle

A good sign that all is in order. Alternatively, it could indicate an interloper in a relationship, either romantic or business.

Wheel

Fortune and chance are involved—generally good fortune.

Windmill

A sign that success will be reached through good, honest effort and sincerity.

Putting It All Together: Doing a Reading

The main thing to appreciate when doing a reading is that your teacup will not give didactic answers. The querent may want to know what they should do in a specific situation; however, the reader does not give a yes or no answer but rather a reading that tells what influences seem to be affecting that situation. The decision is up to the querent, not the reader. And make sure that the querent understands that you are not guaranteeing a result.

Finally, what should you do if asked whether the querent should cross your palm with silver? The tradition is that the querent pays the reader for acting as a conduit between the here and now and the future. A gift is supposed to be made. You may feel that a symbolic gift made by waving a coin over the hand is sufficient. Or you may ask that the querent simply make a gift of a coin to a charity.

And then you are ready to begin the art of tasseography.

Acknowledgments

There are several people that I would like to thank for helping me with The Tea Cyclopedia. First, I would like to thank my wonderful agent, Isabel Atherton, at Creative Authors, who went all the way to New York City and took the proposal for this book with her.

A very big thank you to Julie Matysik, senior editor at Skyhorse, who read the proposal and commissioned the book. I know that she is a tea enthusiast and I like to imagine that Isabel and Julie discussed the proposal over tea.

I am really grateful to my daughter, Kate Barker, for giving me her recipe for Earl Grey Fairy Cakes and for advising and helping me with my research for the chapter on tea cocktails. That was a lot of fun.

And finally, my thanks as always to my wife, Rachel, for all her support over the years. She makes everything so worthwhile.

Notes

1. The UK Tea Council, www.tea.co.uk/teafacts.
2. The Tea Association of the USA, www.teausa.com/14655/tea-fact-sheet.
3. Russell, Jesse and Ronald Cohn, *The Classic of Tea* (Edinburgh: Bookvika Publishing, 2012), 13–15.
4. Pettigrew, Jane, *A Social History of Tea* (London: The National Trust, 2001), 10.
5. Steward, Lori Jane, *The Green Gourmet Perfect Cup Of Tea Book : Tea History and Culture, Teas of the World, Growth and Processing, Blending and Grading, How To Match Tea with Food and How To Make the Perfect Cup of Tea* (Scotts Valley, CA: Amazon digital services, 2012), 8–9.
6. Opplinger, Peter, *Green Tea: The Delicious Everyday Health Drink* (Essex: Saffron Walden, 1996), 22.
7. Saberi, Helen, *Tea: A Global History* (London: Reaktion Books, 2010), 66–80.
8. Freeman, Michael, and Salena Ahmed, *The Tea Horse Road: China's Ancient Trade Road to Tibet* (Bangkok: River Books Press, 2010).
9. Mitchell, Stephen, foreword to *Tao Te Ching* (New York: Harper Perennial Modern Classics, 2006).
10. Russell and Cohn, *The Classic of Tea*, 8.
11. Ibid., 5–7.
12. Ibid., 28.
13. Saberi, *Tea: A Global History*, 74.

14. Latham, Robert, *The Illustrated Pepys Extracts from the Diary* (London: Book Club Assciates,1979), 31.

15. Pettigrew, *A Social History of Tea*, 90–92.

16. Ibid., 15–17.

17. Moxham, Roy, *A Brief History of Tea* (London: Constable & Robinson, 2003), 104–106.

18. Pettigrew, *A Social History of Tea*, 51.

19. Moxham, *A Brief History of Tea*, 7–12.

20. Heiss, Mary Lou, and Robert Heiss, *The Tea Enthusiast's Handbook: A Guide to Enjoying the World's Best Teas* (New York: Ten Speed Press, 2010), 6.

21. Steward, *Perfect Cup of Tea*, 20–22.

22. Heiss and Heiss, *Tea Enthusiast's Handbook*, 40–174.

23. Saberi, *Tea: A Global History*, 22–24.

24. Souter, Keith, *Schoolboy Science Revisited* (Barnsle: Pen & Sword, 2011).

25. Rousmaniere, Leah, *Collecting Teapots* (New York: Random House, 2004), 49–51.

26. Ibid., 65.

27. The Tea Association of the USA.

28. Steward, *Perfect Cup of Tea*, 14.

29. The Tea Association of the USA.

30. Souter, *Schoolboy Science Revisited*, 26–29.

31. Seeram, N. P., S. M. Henning, Y. Niu, et al., "Catechin and caffeine content of green tea dietary supplements and correlation with antioxidant capacity," *Journal of Agricultural and Food Chemistry* 54, no. 5 (2006): 1,599–1,603.

32. Lambert J. D., and C. S. Yang, "Mechanisms of cancer prevention by tea constituents." *Journal of Nutrition* 133, no. 19 (2006): 3262S–3267S.

33. Zaveri N. T., "Green tea and its polyphenolic catechins: Medicinal uses in cancer and noncancer applications," *Life Sciences*, 78, no. 18 (2006): 2,073–2,080.

34. Steele V. E., G. J. Kelloff, D. Balentine, et al., "Comparative chemopreventive mechanisms of green tea, black tea and selected polyphenol extracts measured by in vitro bioassay," *Carcinogenesis* 21, no. 1 (2000): 63–67.

35. Yu Tang Gao, Joseph K. McLaughlin, William J. Blot, et al., "Reduced Risk of Esophageal Cancer Associated With Green Tea Consumption," *J Natl Caner Inst* 86, no. 11 (1994): 855–858.

36. Nechuta, Sarah, Xiao-Ou Shu, Hong-Lan Li, et al., "Prospective cohort study of tea consumption and risk of digestive system cancers: results from the Shanghai Women's Health Study," *AmJ Clin Nutr* 96, no. 5 (November 2012): 1,056–1,063.

37. Li, N., Z. Sun, C. Han, et al., "The chemopreventive effects of tea on human oral precancerous mucosa lesions," *Proceedings from the Society of Experimental Biology and Medicine* 220, no. 4 (1999): 218–224.

38. Hakim, I. A., R. B. Harris, S. Brown, et al., "Effect of increased tea consumption on oxidative DNA damage among smokers: A randomized controlled study," *Journal of Nutrition* 133, no. 10 (2003):3303S–3309S.

39. Kuriyama, S., T. Shimazu, K. Ohmori, et al., "Green tea consumption and mortality due to cardiovascular disease, cancer and all causes in Japan: *The Ohsaki study,*" *JAMA* 296 (2006): 1,255–1,265.

40. Alexopoulos, et al., "The acute effect of green tea consumption on endothelial function in healthy individuals," *European Journal of Cardiovascular Prevention & Rehabilitation* 15, no. 3 (2008): 300.

41. Institute of Food Technologists, "Black Tea May Fight Diabetes, *ScienceDaily* (August 31, 2009).

42. Chu, et al., "Green Tea Catechins and Their Oxidative Protection in the Rat Eye," *Journal of Agricultural and Food Chemistry* 58, no. 3 (2010): 1,523.

43. Vinson, J. A., and Y. A. Dabbagh. "Effect of green and black tea supplementation on lipids, lipid oxidation and fibrinogen in the hamster: mechanisms for the epidemiological benefits of tea drinking," *FEBS Letters*, volume 433, issues 1–2 (1998): 44–46.

44. Nagao, T., Y. Komine, S. Soga, et al., "Ingestion of a tea rich in cate-chins leads to a reduction in body fat and malondialdehyde-modified LDL in men," *Am J Clin Nutr* 81, no.1 (2005): 122–129.

45. Dickens, Charles, *Oliver Twist* (London: Wordsworth Classics, 2000).

46. Dickens, Charles, *Great Expectations* (London: Wordsworth Classics, 2000).

Selected Bibliography

Part One The History of Tea

Carp, Benjamin. *Defiance of the Patriots: The Boston Tea Party and the Making of America*. New Haven, CT: Yale University Press, 2011.

Fay, Peter Ward. *The Opium War*. New edition. Raleigh, University of North Carolina Press, 1998.

Freeman, Michael, and Salena Ahmed. *The Tea Horse Road: China's Ancient Trade Road to Tibet*. Bangkok: River Books Press, 2011.

Griffiths, John. *Tea: A History of the Drink That Changed the World*. Reprint, London: Andre Deutsch, 2011.

Keay, John. *The Honourable Company: A history of the English East India Company*. London: HarperCollins, 1993.

Latham, Robert. *The Illustrated Pepys Extracts from the Diary*. London: Book Club Associates, 1979.

MacFarlane, Alan. *The Empire of Tea: The Remarkable History of the Plant that Took Over the World*. New York: Overlook Press, 2009.

Mitchell, Stephen. *Tao Te Ching*. London: Frances Lincoln, 1999.

Moxham, Roy. *A Brief History of Tea*. London: Constable & Robinson, 2003.

Okakura, Kakuzo. *The Book of Tea*. London: Penguin Classic Edition, 2010.

Pettigrew, Jane. *A Social History of Tea*. London: The National Trust, 2001.

Rose, Sarah. *For All the Tea in China: Espionage, Empire and the Secret Formula for the World's Favourite Drink*. London: Arrow, 2010.

Russell, Jesse, and Ronald Cohn. *The Classic of Tea*. Edinburgh: Bookvika Publishing, 2012.

Saberi, Helen. *Tea: A Global History*. London: Reaktion Books, 2010.

Tomalin, Claire. *Samuel Pepys: the Unequalled Self*. London: Viking, 2002.

Part Two Taking Tea

Caldicott, Carolyn. *Vintage Tea Party*. London: Francis Lincoln, 2012.

Clark, Garth. *The Artful Teapot*. London: Thames & Hudson, 2001.

Clark, Garth. *The Eccentric Teapot: Four Hundred Years of Invention*. New York: Abeyville Press, 1989.

Heiss, Mary Lou, and Robert Heiss. *The Tea Enthusiast's Handbook: A Guide to Enjoying the World's Best Teas*. New York: Ten Speed Press, 2010.

Langley, Andrew. *The Little Book of Tea Tips*. Bath: Absolute Press, 2005.

Mathie, Johanna. *Scottish Teatime Recipes*. Sevenoaks: Salmon Ltd, 1998.

Pnk Guru Tea Scientist. *Tea Taster: How to Become a Tea Taster?: with Scientific Tea Testing Tasting and Blending Techniques?*. Scotts Valley, CA: CreateSpace Independent Publishing Platform, 2011.

Rousmaniere, Leah. *Collecting Teapots*. New York: Random House, 2004.

Simpson, Helen. *The Ritz London Book of Afternoon Tea: The Art and Pleasures of Taking Tea*. London: Ebury Press, 2006.

Steward, Lori Jane. *The Green Gourmet Perfect Cup Of Tea Book : Tea History and Culture, Teas of the World, Growth and Processing, Blending and Grading, How To Match Tea with Food and How To Make the Perfect Cup of Tea*. Scotts Valley, CA: Amazon digital services, 2012.

Zak, Victoria. *20,000 Secrets of Tea: The most effective ways to benefit from nature's healing herbs*. New York: Dell, 2000.

Part Three Using Tea

Claflin, Edward. *Age Protectors*. Emmaus, PA: Rodale Press, 1998.

Cross, Robert. *The Classic 1000 Cocktails*. London: W Foulsham & Co, 2003.

Davies, Stephen, and Alan Stewart. *Nutritional Medicine: The Drug-Free Guide to Better Family Health*. London: Pan, 1987.

Dickens, Charles. *Great Expectations*. London: Wordsworth Classics, 1992.

Dickens, Charles. *Oliver Twist*. London: Wordsworth Classics, 2000.

Fenton, Sasha. *Fortune-telling by Tea Leaves: a Practical Guide to the Ancient Art of Tasseography.* Wellingborough: Thorsons, 1996.

Gibson, Walter, and Litzka Gibson. *The Complete Illustrated Book of Divination & Prophecy*. London: Souvenir Press, 1987.

Kirschmann, John. *Nutritional Almanac*. New York: McGraw-Hill, 1984.

McNulty, Henry. *One For The Road: Vogue Guide to Non Alcoholic Drinks*. London: Hamlyn, 1986.

Minetta. *Tea-Cup Fortune Telling*. London: Foulsham, 1960.

Moray, Keith. *Flotsam and Jetsam*. London: Hale, 2010.

Opplinger, Peter. *Green Tea: The Delicious Everyday Health Drink*. Saffron Walden, 1997.

Orczy, Baroness. *Old Man in the Corner*. House of Stratus, new edition, 2008.

Osborne, Charles. *The Life and Crimes of Agatha Christie*. London: HarperCollins, 2000.

Regan, Gary. *The Joy of Mixology: The Consummate Guide to the Bartender's Craft*. New York: Random House, 2004.

Reynolds, Virginia. *The Little Black Book of Cocktails*. London: Peter Pauper Press, 2003.

Robinson, Stearn, and Tom Corbett. *The Dreamer's Dictionary*. London: HarperCollins, 1993.

Snow, Charles Percy. *Death Under Sail*. New edition, Cornwall: House of Stratus, 2008.

Souter, Keith. *Schoolboy Science Revisited*. Barnsley: Pen & Sword, 2011.

This, Herve. *Kitchen Mysteries: Revealing the Science of Cooking*. Translated by Jody Gladding. New York: Columbia University Press, 2007.

Van Gulik, Robert. *The Chinese Maze Murders*. London: Panther, 1962.

Wagstaff, Virginia, and Stephen Poole. *Agatha Christie: A Reader's Companion*. London: Aurum Press, 2007.

Ward, James. *Dreams and Omens*. London: Foulsham, 1963.

Useful Websites

Jing Tea

This is a tea and teaware supplier. The website contains a wealth of information about the different types of tea.

JING Tea Ltd
London Head Office
Canterbury Court
London
SW9 6DE
United Kingdom
www.jingtea.com

Lipton

This company was started in 1880, by Thomas Lipton. It is now one of the world's leading tea brands.
www.liptontea.com

The Tea Association of the USA

This organization promotes tea consumption and has an international database for statistics, production, and consumption. It has a wealth of useful material.

The Tea Association of the USA
Suite 801
362 Fifth Avenue
New York, NY 10001
Email: info@teausa.com
www.teausa.com

The Tea Palace

This is a company with two stores in London. They supply some of the finest teas in the world from India, Sri Lanka, China, Japan, and Taiwan.

The Tea Palace
9a-9b Imperial Studios
Imperial Road
London
SW6 2AG
Email: info@teapalace.co.uk
www.teapalace.co.uk

UK Tea Council

This organization has a wealth of information about all aspects of tea.

The United Kingdom Tea Council Ltd.
Suite 10, Fourth Floor
Crown House
One Crown Square
Woking
GU21 6HR
www.tea.co.uk

Wissotzky Tea

The leading producer and exporter of tea in Israel, the company was founded in 1849, in Russia. This website has a wealth of information about tea's history, tea grading, and tea tasting.

Wissotzky house,
103 Hashmonaim st.
POB 147
61001 Tel Aviv
Israel
Email: oritc@wtea.com
www.wtea.com

Index